First World War
and Army of Occupation
War Diary
France, Belgium and Germany

39 DIVISION
Divisional Troops
186 Brigade Royal Field Artillery
5 March 1916 - 17 December 1918

WO95/2574/5

The Naval & Military Press Ltd
www.nmarchive.com
Published in association with The National Archives

Published by

The Naval & Military Press Ltd

Unit 10 Ridgewood Industrial Park,

Uckfield, East Sussex,

TN22 5QE England

Tel: +44 (0) 1825 749494

www.naval-military-press.com

www.nmarchive.com

This diary has been reprinted in facsimile from the original. Any imperfections are inevitably reproduced and the quality may fall short of modern type and cartographic standards.

© **Crown Copyright**
Images reproduced by permission of The National Archives, London, England, 2015.

Contents

Document type	Place/Title	Date From	Date To
Heading	WO95/2574 Mar 16-Dec 18 186 Bde RFA		
Heading	186th Brigade R.F.A. Mar 1916-Dec 1918		
Miscellaneous	186 Brig R F A Vol I		
Heading	186th Brigade Royal Field Artillery March 1916		
Miscellaneous	Milford	05/03/1916	05/03/1916
War Diary	Southampton	05/03/1916	05/03/1916
War Diary	Havre	06/03/1916	07/03/1916
War Diary	Thiennes	08/03/1916	08/03/1916
War Diary	Lynde	09/03/1916	09/03/1916
War Diary	Bleu	13/03/1916	13/03/1916
War Diary	Sailly Sur Lys	24/03/1916	26/03/1916
War Diary	Guarbecque	29/03/1916	31/03/1916
Heading	186th Brigade Royal Field Artillery April 1916		
War Diary	Guarbecque	01/04/1916	30/04/1916
Heading	186th Brigade Royal Field Artillery May 1916		
Miscellaneous	D.A.G. 3rd Echelon	01/06/1916	01/06/1916
War Diary	Machin	01/05/1916	31/05/1916
Heading	186th Brigade Royal Field Artillery June 1916		
War Diary	Festubert	17/06/1916	17/06/1916
Heading	186th Brigade Royal Field Artillery July 1916		
War Diary	Loisne	01/07/1916	26/07/1916
War Diary	Locon	27/07/1916	31/07/1916
Heading	186th Brigade Royal Field Artillery August 1916		
Miscellaneous	Headquarters 39th Division.	01/09/1916	01/09/1916
War Diary	Locon	01/08/1916	31/08/1916
Heading	186th Brigade Royal Field Artillery September 1916		
War Diary	Englebelmer	01/09/1916	23/09/1916
Heading	186th Brigade Royal Field Artillery October 1916		
War Diary	Bus	01/10/1916	03/10/1916
War Diary	Hedeauville	04/10/1916	31/10/1916
Heading	186th Brigade Royal Field Artillery November 1916		
War Diary	Hedeauville	01/11/1916	30/11/1916
Heading	186th Brigade Royal Field Artillery December 1916		
War Diary	Ochtezeele	01/12/1916	31/12/1916
Heading	War Diary 186 Brigade RFA Volume 2		
War Diary	Troistours	01/01/1917	30/01/1917
War Diary	Ypres	02/02/1917	28/02/1917
Heading	War Diary Volume II 186 Brigade RFA		
War Diary	Ypres	01/03/1917	20/04/1917
War Diary	Herzeele	21/04/1917	29/04/1917
Miscellaneous	39th Divisional Artillery	09/04/1917	09/04/1917
War Diary	Herzeele	03/05/1917	03/05/1917
War Diary	Noordpeene	04/05/1917	04/05/1917
War Diary	Polincove	05/05/1917	17/05/1917
War Diary	Rubrouck	18/05/1918	18/05/1918
War Diary	Herzeele	20/05/1917	26/05/1917
War Diary	Reigersburg	28/05/1917	29/06/1917
Miscellaneous	Casualties		
War Diary	Lock 7	01/10/1917	25/10/1917
Miscellaneous	Casualties Appendix 11	31/10/1917	31/10/1917

Miscellaneous	Honours And Awards Appendix 10	31/10/1917	31/10/1917
War Diary	Manor Farm	01/11/1917	28/11/1917
Miscellaneous	Casualties	30/11/1917	30/11/1917
Miscellaneous	Casualties Appendix 13		
War Diary		18/11/1917	18/11/1917
War Diary	Vlamertinghe	21/11/1917	05/12/1917
War Diary	28 D.25.a.95.45	07/12/1917	07/12/1917
War Diary	Low Farm	07/12/1917	21/12/1917
War Diary	Vlamertinghe	22/12/1917	22/12/1917
Miscellaneous	39th Divisional Artillery Table Of Reliefs Appendix 1		
Miscellaneous	King's Birthday Honours Gazette-1917		
Miscellaneous	War Diary 186 Brigade RFA Sheets 23 & 24 Volume II		
War Diary	H.5.d.	08/01/1918	08/01/1918
War Diary	Alberta	11/01/1918	12/01/1918
War Diary	Ypres	02/01/1918	02/01/1918
War Diary	Alberta	10/01/1918	23/01/1918
War Diary	Steenje Mill	25/01/1918	28/01/1918
War Diary	Lanoove Ville	30/01/1918	30/01/1918
Miscellaneous	Casualties		
War Diary	Lancuville	02/02/1918	02/02/1918
War Diary	Allaines	03/02/1918	03/02/1918
War Diary	Moislains	12/02/1918	13/02/1918
War Diary	Nurlu	16/02/1918	17/02/1918
War Diary	Heudicourt	21/02/1918	01/03/1918
Miscellaneous	186th Brigade R.F.A. War Diary Pages 19 & 20 Volume II		
Heading	Headquarters 186th Brigade R.F.A. March 1918		
War Diary	Heudecourt	01/03/1918	11/03/1918
War Diary	Halle	14/03/1918	15/03/1918
War Diary	Haot Allaines	15/03/1918	21/03/1918
War Diary	Bois De Tincourt	22/03/1918	22/03/1918
War Diary	Bussu	23/03/1918	23/03/1918
War Diary	Herbecourt	24/03/1918	25/03/1918
War Diary	Cappy	26/03/1918	26/03/1918
War Diary	Morcourt	27/03/1918	27/03/1918
War Diary	Villers Brettoneux	30/03/1918	31/03/1918
Miscellaneous	Appendix 15 Casualties.		
Miscellaneous	186th Brigade R.F.A. April 1918		
War Diary	Villers Bret (Prisoners Cage)	04/04/1918	04/04/1918
War Diary	Bois L'Abbe	05/04/1918	13/04/1918
War Diary	Cagny	15/04/1918	15/04/1918
War Diary	Behencourt	16/04/1918	16/04/1918
War Diary	Saulty	17/04/1918	17/04/1918
Miscellaneous	Casualties April		
Miscellaneous	Copy	14/04/1918	14/04/1918
War Diary	Hauteville	30/04/1918	01/06/1918
War Diary	Agny	02/06/1918	15/06/1918
War Diary	Beaumetz	24/06/1918	27/06/1918
War Diary	Beaumetz	05/06/1918	22/06/1918
War Diary	Pas	25/06/1918	25/06/1918
War Diary	Couin	25/06/1918	03/07/1918
War Diary	St Jan Ter Biezen	04/07/1918	07/07/1918
War Diary	Vlamertinghe	14/07/1918	14/07/1918
War Diary	Vlamertinghe Chateau	16/07/1918	01/08/1918
Miscellaneous	Casualties	31/07/1918	31/07/1918
War Diary	Droglandt	05/08/1918	05/08/1918

War Diary	Belle Croix	06/08/1918	15/08/1918
War Diary	Fletre	15/08/1918	21/08/1918
War Diary	La Breade	22/08/1918	23/08/1918
War Diary	ACQ	23/08/1918	24/08/1918
War Diary	Arras	25/08/1918	26/08/1918
War Diary	Tilloy H.35.c.8.6	27/08/1918	27/08/1918
War Diary	Wancourt	28/08/1918	31/08/1918
Miscellaneous	Appendix 19 Casualties		
War Diary	Cherisy	01/09/1918	01/09/1918
War Diary	V. 6b.80.30	02/09/1918	02/09/1918
War Diary	W.10.b.5.5.	13/09/1918	14/09/1918
War Diary	Arras	22/09/1918	22/09/1918
War Diary	Buissy		
War Diary	W. 23.d		
Miscellaneous	Appendix 21 Casualties	30/09/1918	30/09/1918
War Diary		05/10/1918	30/10/1918
Miscellaneous	Casualties For October		
War Diary	Maing	01/11/1918	04/11/1918
War Diary	Faumont	04/11/1918	30/11/1918
Miscellaneous	Appendix 24 Honours Awards		
War Diary	Faumont	17/12/1918	17/12/1918

WO 95/2574
Mai '16 – Dec '18
186 Bde RFA

39TH DIVISION
DIVL ARTILLERY

186TH BRIGADE R.F.A.

MAR 1916 - DEC 1918.

(Missing Feb '17
Jul/Aug & Sept '17)

39

186 Bry
RFA

Vol 1

39th Divisiona;.Artillery.

Brigade disembarked HAVRE 6.3.16

186th BRIGADE

ROYAL FIELD ARTILLERY.

MARCH 1 9 1 6

Dec 1918

Army Form C. 2118

WAR DIARY
or
INTELLIGENCE SUMMARY
(Erase heading not required.)

Instructions regarding War Diaries and Intelligence Summaries are contained in F.S. Regs., Part II. and the Staff Manual respectively. Title Pages will be prepared in manuscript.

Place	Date	Hour	Summary of Events and Information	Remarks and references to Appendices
			186 BRIGADE R.F.A.	
MILFORD	5/3/16		Entrained for port of Embarkation	"A" By find its Forefeet on 16/3 (Major C. PHILLIPS)
SOUTHAMPTON			Arrived & Embarked	B 18/3 (2/L R.J. O'CONNELL)
HAVRE	6/3/16		Disembarked & proceeded to a rest camp	C 18/3 (Capt A. HANCOCKS)
	7/3/16		Entrained	D 18/3 (Capt J.V. SAUNDERSON)
THIENNES	8/3/16		Detrained & marched to billets at LYNDE remaining there till 11/3	
			2/Lt R.E. BOWES thrown from his horse & injured. Evacuated to ENGLAND & struck off strength of "D" Battery on 16.3.16	
LYNDE	9/3/16			
	12/3/16		Marched to BLEU - leaving LYNDE at 8.30 am & arriving at BLEU at 3.30 pm killed	
BLEU	13/3/16		Hd Qrs marched to SAILLY-SUR-LYS. "A" Battery into action 1000 S of LAVENTIE	
			Am Col " " HAIES LE BAS B+D " 1 mile N "	B+D 2 guns
			C " " " " fired E of FLEURBAIX (ELBOW FARM)	forty in action
			Batteries withdrawn from action to began line on night of 23rd March 1916	
SAILLY SUR LYS	24/3/16		2/Lt L. HORDERN joined "A" Bty - On 18-3-16 2/Lt A VALE joined "D" Bty. On 26/3 2/Lt G.S. MILLAR joined "C" By	
	26/3/16		Marched to billets at GUARBECQUE	
GUARBECQUE	27/3/16		Lieut HAYLER joined & assumed command of B Battery	
	28+31/3/16		Resting at GUARBECQUE	

C. W. Deer
Comdg 186 Brigade R.F.A.

39th Divisional Artillery.

186th BRIGADE

ROYAL FIELD ARTILLERY

APRIL 1916:

186 RFA
Vol 2

WAR DIARY
or
INTELLIGENCE SUMMARY
(Erase heading not required.)

Army Form C. 2118.
XXXIX

Place	Date	Hour	Summary of Events and Information	Remarks and references to Appendices
GUARBECQUE	APRIL 1916 1 & 2		186 BRIGADE RFA	
			Resting till 15th	
	3		4 Offrs & 60 men attached to 33rd Div Arty for instruction	
	4		2/Lt G.C. PROBERT joined & posted to "C" By	
	9		Another party of 4 Offrs & 60 men to 33rd Div Arty - 1st party returned	
	16		A, B & D Batteries into action	BETHUNE bombing sheet
			A at F5 C 35	36 A.SE.
			B at X 24 C 24	36 SW.
			D at F5 C 05	36 B NE
			C Bty & rest billeted at W8 D 83 till 29th Moved to Q29 D77	36 C NW.
			A.C. at billet W 21 D 60 - later at Q 36 A 82	
	20 24		2/Lt H.A. DUNKLEY to ENGLAND (Sick)	
	21st to 30th		2/Lt YOUNG joined & posted to "A" Bty	
			Work as above.	Cooperating for RA Comdg 1st Brigade RFA

39th Divisional Artillery.

186th BRIGADE

ROYAL FIELD ARTILLERY.

M A Y   1 9 1 6:

D.A.G 3rd Echelon
— Herewith from Diary for
the month of May 1916

C H Kilnen Lt Col XXX
1.6.16 Comdg 12 Bn XXX

WAR DIARY or INTELLIGENCE SUMMARY

186 RFA Army Form C. 2118
Vol 3

XXXIX

Place	Date	Hour	Summary of Events and Information	Remarks and references to Appendices
In action	May 1916		186 Brigade R.F.A	
	1		Capt. J. HERON joined & assumed command of "D" By	
	3		2/Lt W F MOUNT joined & posted to "B" By	
	17		Brigade Hd Qr Staff moved from 179 Hd Bde at LOISNE	
			2nd Lt CARLIER assumed command of "C" Group 39th Div Arty	
	20		The divisional artillery has been reorganized to that each brigade consists of 3 - 18 pdr batteries & 1 4.5 Howitzer Battery	X B/174
			A/186 became D/174 B/174 became A/186	
			B/186 " D/179 B/66 " B/66	
			C/186 " D/164 C/164 " C/66	
			C/179 " C/86	
			The R.H.C. has broken up its ducks being performed by the D.H.C.	
			Which has also re-organized	
	29	10 AM	C Groups were placed under orders of R.S.H.A 36th Division	
	30 31		the same type Group	
			In action	Carrivan Lt Col RA
				Comdg 186 Brigade R.F.A

39th Divisional Artillery.

186th BRIGADE

ROYAL FIELD ARTILLERY.

JUNE 1916

Army Form C. 2118

186 R.F.A

Vol 4

WAR DIARY
INTELLIGENCE SUMMARY
(Erase heading not required.)

Place	Date	Hour	Summary of Events and Information	Remarks and references to Appendices
FESTUBERT	June 1916	17.	186 Brigade R.F.A. A & B Batteries left "C" Group for F (FERME DU BOIS) & took over gun positions from 35th Div Arty - "A" Bty at S.1.d.4.8. "B" Bty at M.26.a.3.0. "C" Bty was transferred to B (GIVENCHY) Group. 332 Div Arty - It did not change its position.	

M Brown
Lt Col RA
Comdg 186 Brigade R.F.A.

39th Divisional Artillery.

186th BRIGADE

ROYAL FIELD ARTILLERY.

JULY 1916

K063

Army Form C. 2118

WAR DIARY
or
INTELLIGENCE SUMMARY
(Erase heading not required.)

Vol I No 5
From 1st to 31st July 1916

Instructions regarding War Diaries and Intelligence Summaries are contained in F.S. Regs., Part II. and the Staff Manual respectively. Title Pages will be prepared in manuscript.

Place	Date	Hour	Summary of Events and Information	Remarks and references to Appendices
	1916		186 Brigade RA	
LOISNE	July 1st	7b	Hd Qrs in charge of FESTUBERT group, 39 Div Army. Relieved by Hd Qrs 179 Bde RA at 12 noon 7b.	
	1st	7b	Do red Nat LOCON.	
			A B C 1st Bdes in action A B K GIVENCHY groups, D by FESTUBERT group	
			D Bty to rest at HINGES on 25th	
LOCON	31	31	Hd Qrs & Btys resting	
			A C & D Btys in action in FESTUBERT group	

Williams
Lt Col RA
Comdg 186 Brigade RA

39th Divisional Artillery.

186th BRIGADE

ROYAL FIELD ARTILLERY.

AUGUST 1 9 1 6

RA/29/G

Headquarters
39th Division

Herewith War Diary
106th Brigade R.F.A. plans

[signature]
Brigadier General,
G.O.C. R.A. 39th Division.

WAR DIARY / INTELLIGENCE SUMMARY

Army Form C. 2118
VOL I No 6
186 RFA

Place	Date	Hour	Summary of Events and Information	Remarks and references to Appendices
LOCON	August 1916		**186 Brigade RFA**	
	1-9		Hd Qrs in rest. "B" Battery in action on 1/8/16 in FESTUBERT group. "A" Battery to rest at HINGES	
	10		Hd Qrs & "A" Bty marched to LES PESSES – distance 17 miles – in billets	
	11		B C & D Btys joined Hd Qrs & marched from FESTUBERT group – in billets	
	12		The brigade marched to ST MICHEL – Picquigny – distance 14 miles	
	13-20		Batteries training in training area	
	21		Brigade marched to LUCHEUX – Picquigny – distance 16 miles	
	22		" " " THIEVRES – " 7 "	
	23-24		Resting	
	25		Brigade marched to BERTRANCOURT – in billets – distance 7 miles	
	26		A Bty & ½ C Bty, under Major NICHOLSON, in action in MESNIL VALLEY } Wagon lines at BERTRANCOURT
			B Bty & ½ C Bty, under CAPT KEMP in action, pointed SE of ENGLEBELMER
			D Bty under CAPT HERON in action at SE corner of VIZERNONT WOOD
			Lt Col KILNER, with Brigade Hd Qrs, in command of "K" group. 39 off. consisting of 4 C, ½ D Bty of 191 Bde – D Bty 179 Bde & "A" Bty 156 Bde. Total 16 18pdrs & 8 4.5 Howrs	
	30		Batteries registering & carrying out minor operations	
			2nd Lieut WINDMILLS fever 4th Bty of 3rd Divn & A WILSON joined D Bty C.W.Kilner Lt Col RFA Comdg 186 Brigade RFA

39th Divisional Artillery.

186th BRIGADE

ROYAL FIELD ARTILLERY.

SEPTEMBER 1 9 1 6

Army Form C. 2118

WAR DIARY
or
INTELLIGENCE SUMMARY
(Erase heading not required.)

VOL. 1. Vol 7 39 Days

Place	Date	Hour	Summary of Events and Information	Remarks and references to Appendices
ENGLEBELMER	September 1st 3rd		186th Brigade R.F.A	
			Lt. F.D. ODELL wounded - D/186 Heavily shelled - Officers Kits destroyed Battery opened fire at 5·10 am and ceased about 1·30 pm taking part in an organised attack chiefly N. of the RIVER ANCRE - A/186 shelled all night + Mrs NICHOLSON slightly wounded (at duty)	
	4th 5th 6th		A/186 C. Wagon fire A/186 into action Q.26d.1.5½ Lt Col CH KILNER assumed responsibility for line from Q.17.6.0.5 to RIVER ANCRE Maj NICHOLSON to 13th Field Ambulance. CAPT ISANDON assumed the command of A By	
	7th 8th 9th		Group Headquarters shelled by Lone Shells from 10pm to 4am Group Headquarters moved to P.24.d.8.7 D/186 moved to Q.34.c.6½.7	
	14th 15th 21st 23rd		LtCol CA KILNER to BUS lick - ½Col C RUDKIN assumes Command of Group M) MAITED opened and tent drawn Lt Col J ALLARDYCE to BUS to rest A.D.V. and all the Staff of 186 Headquarters to BUS to rest	

CH Kilner LtCol
Fc 186 Bde R.F.A

1875 Wt. W593/826 1,000,000 4/15 J.B.C. & A. A.D.S.S./Forms/C. 2118.

39th Divisional Artillery.

186th BRIGADE

ROYAL FIELD ARTILLERY.

OCTOBER 1 9 1 6

186 "Brigade" R.F.A.

Vol 8
No 8
Army Form C. 2118
VOL 1
Period 1st - 31st October 1916

WAR DIARY
INTELLIGENCE SUMMARY
Summary of Events and Information

186 BRIGADE R.F.A.

Place	Date	Hour	Summary of Events and Information	Remarks and references to Appendices
	October 1916			
BUS	1-3		Hd Qrs & battery wagon lines at BUS	
HEDAUVILLE	4		Above to HEDAUVILLE in Bivouac	
	15		Relieved Hd Qrs Right Group (17th Brigade RFA)	
	16		Hd Qrs to rest. All moves cancelled except "C" Battery which relieved "A" Battery 17th Brigade R.A. in action in MESNIL VALLEY	
	20		"A" Battery to new position in MESNIL VALLEY	
	31		A, B & C Batteries in action in MESNIL VALLEY & "D" Battery in AVELUY WOOD	

Carisbrooke
Brig Gen RFA
Comdg 186 Brigade RFA

39th Divisional Artillery.

186th BRIGADE

ROYAL FIELD ARTILLERY.

NOVEMBER 1 9 1 6

WAR DIARY
or
INTELLIGENCE SUMMARY

186 Bde R.F.A. Army Form C. 2118 No 9 32nd

Vol 1. Sh 9

Place	Date	Hour	Summary of Events and Information	Remarks and references to Appendices
MESNIL			**186 Brigade R.F.A.**	
	NOVEMBER 1916			
	11/16 to 17/16		Hd Qrs at rest – A.B.&C Batteries in action in MESNIL VALLEY D Battery in action in AVELUY WOOD. *Lieut H SEWELL "C" By killed in action on 13th	
	18/16		Hd Qrs took over "A" Group 39th Div.Arty from 174th Brigade R.F.A. 37th Divison	
	19/16		Hd Qrs to rest at HEDEAUVILLE handing over to 175th Bde RFA	
	19/16		Hd Qrs & A,B,C & D Batteries withdrawn from the line on 19/16	
	20/16		marched to ORVILLE – distance 16 miles & billeted	
	23/16		to BUSERS sur CANCHE – 17 miles & billeted	
	24/16		to HUCLIERS – 17 miles – billeted & rested till 25/16	
	25/16		to AUCHY AU BOIS, distance 14 miles & billeted	
	26/16		to THIENNES, distance 11 miles & billeted	
	27/16		to OCHTEZEELE, distance 17 miles & billeted	
			Joined VIII Corps.	
	28/16 to 30.		Resting & re-organizing to 3. 6 gun 18pdr Btys & 1 How 4.5 By. "C" By being continued 186 Brig RFA	

39th Divisional Artillery.

186th BRIGADE

ROYAL FIELD ARTILLERY.

DECEMBER 1 9 1 6

WAR DIARY
INTELLIGENCE SUMMARY

186 Bde RFA Feb 10
Vol 10

Army Form c. 2118

Place	Date	Hour	Summary of Events and Information	Remarks and references to Appendices
OOSTERZEELE	Feb 1916		**186 Brigade RFA**	
	1		C. Battery 184 Brigade RFA joined & became C/186. Brigade now consisting of 3 – 6 gun 18 pdr batteries & 1 – 4 How & 5 Battery. Battery Commanders being A – Major W. SNICHOLSON B – Acty Major G.C. KEMP? C – Major F.E. SPENCER M.C. D – Capt G. HERON	
	9		Inspected by Lt Gen Sir AYLMER HUNTER WESTON Comdg VIII Corps	
	15		" " Gen Sir HERBERT PLUMER Comdg 2nd Army	
	17		Hd Qrs relieved 119th Bde H.Q. at TROIS TOURS CHATEAU (J 29 a 55.35) (means Extract Group Sheet 27) A Bty relieved A 119 at J 22 d 1.8 – 3 Bty relieved B119 at J22 + 6 + C26 C315 -do- C Bty relieved B119 at J13 d 7.7 + B14 49 + D Bty relieved D119 at J22 d 7.0 -do- C/119 at I 2.c 8.2 (Sheet 28) under orders of Corps group commander Lt.Col CHRISTNER	
	31		In action	encirceurs

Comdg 186 Brigade RFA

Lt Col RA

Comdg 186 Brigade RFA

Vol 20

War Diary
186 Brigade R.F.A.

Volume 2

Army Form C. 2118

186 Bde R.F.A
Vol 2 No 1
Vol XI

WAR DIARY or INTELLIGENCE SUMMARY

Place	Date	Hour	Summary of Events and Information	Remarks and references to Appendices
TROIS TURS	January 1917		186 Brigade R.F.A.	
	1-16		H.Q. & Batteries in action	
	17		1 Section of each battery to new positions N.W. of YPRES	
	18		H.Q. Bde retired H.Q. 277 Brigade R.F.A. at SALVATION CORNER. T.28.d.1½.4½. Sheet 28 NW 1/20000 Remaining sections of batteries to new positions. Batteries in action as follows:-	
			A/186 at I.7.b/.3 9/186 T.7.b.4.9	
			B/186 at I.1.d.9½.4 D/186 T.1.d.5.5	
			L.Col. E.H. KILNER in command of LEFT GROUP 39 Dn. consisting of A, B, C, D/186 and D/293 Brigade	
			C/186 became at 6 a.m.5 How? Battery, receiving 1 section from C/117 Bde and 1 section of 18 pdrs C/117 attached to A/186	
			On 17th the groups were reinforced by 1 9.gun 18 pdr Bty B/117	
				W. Hockett
				L. Col R.A.
				Comdg 186 Brigade R.F.A

Volume II Page 1

WAR DIARY
or
INTELLIGENCE SUMMARY

186 Brigade R.F.A.

Vol 12

Army Form C. 2118

Place	Date	Hour	Summary of Events and Information	Remarks and references to Appendices
YPRES	2/7/17		D/186 Two O.R. wounded	
" "	11/7/17		A/186 Captain KILKELLY slightly wounded and remained at duty. Two other ranks gassed, two O.R. wounded, Lieut A.S. BARNES slightly wounded and remained at duty.	
" "	13/7/17		A/186 Captain E.R.C. KILKELLY wounded and wounded, two O.R. wounded. C/186 Two O.R. wounded	
" "	14/7/17		H.Q. 186 Brigade R.F.A. one O.R. wounded	
" "	15/7/17		B/186 Two O.R. wounded	
" "	15/7/17		Lieut E.W. CLARKE vacated the appointment of adjutant on proceeding to A/186 as second in command. Lieut V. HILL joined from 39th D.A.C. and assumed the duties of adjutant.	
" "	16/7/17		C/186 heavily shelled from 1.45 PM to 2.35 PM. Two guns disabled. No casualties. Lieut F. WILDE gassed and evacuated to D/186.	
" "	18/7/17		The 186 Brigade R.F.A. was relieved by the 296 Brigade R.F.A. 35th Division and moved to the Reserve Area at HOUTKERQUE	Ref map FRANCE sheet 27
" "	19/7/17		and HERZEELE with Brigade H.Q. at E2.d.2. 10.97	A/186 - D10c 45.35 B/186 - D10c 60.50 C/186 - E2.d. 8.9 D/186 - E14c 2.3

Volume II Page 2

Army Form C. 2118

WAR DIARY
or
INTELLIGENCE SUMMARY
186 Brigade R.F.A.
39th Division

(Erase heading not required.)

Instructions regarding War Diaries and Intelligence Summaries are contained in F.S. Regs., Part II. and the Staff Manual respectively. Title Pages will be prepared in manuscript.

Place	Date	Hour	Summary of Events and Information	Remarks and references to Appendices
YPRES	28.2.17	8 pm	The 186 Brigade R.F.A. relieved the 102 Brigade R.F.A. 23rd Division and became Left Group 39th Divisional Artillery with H.Q. at J.14.b.1.8. A/186 J.6.d.3.0.4.5. B/186 J.8.d.3.7. D/186 J.8.c.8.3. 1 Sec C/186 J.3.d.6.5.5.3.	Ref map Sheet FRANCE 28 APPENDIX 1

C.M. Milwad
Lt. R.F.A.
Cmdg 186 Brigade R.F.A.

vol 13

War Diary
Page 3rd
Volume II

186 Brigade RFA

Sheet 3
Volume II

Army Form C. 2118

WAR DIARY
or
INTELLIGENCE SUMMARY 186 Bde R.F.A.
(Erase heading not required.)

Instructions regarding War Diaries and Intelligence Summaries are contained in F.S. Regs., Part II. and the Staff Manual respectively. Title Pages will be prepared in manuscript.

Place	Date	Hour	Summary of Events and Information	Remarks and references to Appendices
YPRES	1/3/17		C/186 one man killed, four other ranks wounded.	
	4/3/17	7.21 p.m.	A call for assistance was received from Right Group 55th D.A. on our left, this was given by A/186, B/186 and D/186, orders to stop firing were given at 7.26 p.m. It transpired that the Boche had blown a mine.	
	9/3/17	7 p.m.	The Boche blew a mine on the front held by 55th Division and a call for support was received from Right Group 55th D.A. This was given by A/186 and B/186. Firing was stopped at 7.50 p.m.	
	12/3/17		Lieut O.N.MASH evacuated to England.	
	13/3/17	6.45 to 9.25 p.m.	The gun positions of A/186 and B/186 were heavily shelled with 10 c.m. 15 c.m. and 77 m.m guns and howitzers. About 150 shell in all, very little damage and no casualities.	
	13/3/17		Lieut O.N.MASH evacuated to England, sick, and struck off the strength.	
	15/3/17		Lt-Colonel C.H.Kilner proceeded on three weeks leave. Major F.E.Spencer assumed command of the 186th Brigade, R.F.A.	
	18/3/17		Lieut H.G.Garland posted to 39th D.A.C.	
	21/3/17		C/186 one Sergeant wounded.	

Army Form C. 2118

Volume 4
Sheet 4

WAR DIARY
or
INTELLIGENCE SUMMARY
186 Brigade RFA

(Erase heading not required.)

Instructions regarding War Diaries and Intelligence Summaries are contained in F. S. Regs., Part II. and the Staff Manual respectively. Title Pages will be prepared in manuscript.

Place	Date	Hour	Summary of Events and Information	Remarks and references to Appendices
YPRES 60452	26/3/17	12.35 a.m.	S.O.S. was sent up by K.R.R. Battalion on our Right Front the guns of the group at once opened fire. On enquiries being made, it was found that all was quiet on the Left Battalion Front, one section of B/186 was then turned on to help the Right, two sections and three guns of D/186 ceased firing. At 1.35 a.m. the front of the Right Battalion was reported clear and the remainder of the guns stopped firing. It transpired that a raid had been attempted by the enemy, but it was unsuccessful.	
	26/3/17		Military Medal awarded to Sgt C. Walton and Sgt Jellyman for rescuing wounded men under heavy shell fire, and to Bdr Rooney for gallant conduct when his battery was being heavily shelled.	
	27/3/17		B/186 gun position heavily shelled with 15 c.m. 10 c.m. and 77 m.m. guns and howitzers from 12.15 p.m. to 8 p.m. 2/Lt S. H. Freeman slightly wounded and remained at duty.	
	27/3/17		One man slightly wounded	

J. R. Hencen
Major RFA
Comd., 186th Brigade, R. F. A.

Army Form C. 2118

WAR DIARY
or
INTELLIGENCE SUMMARY
(Erase heading not required.)

Sheet 5   Volume 2.

Instructions regarding War Diaries and Intelligence Summaries are contained in F.S. Regs., Part II. and the Staff Manual respectively. Title Pages will be prepared in manuscript.

186 Bde R.F.A.

Vol 14

Place	Date	Hour	Summary of Events and Information	Remarks and references to Appendices
YPRES	7/4/17		Lt-Colonel Kilner rejoined from leave and assumed Command of Left Group.	
"	9/4/17	4.57	Received a call for assistance from the Group on our Right who were being raided, responded with A/186, all quiet at 8 p.m.	
"	10/4/17		Right Group 39th Divisional Artillery relieved by 33rd Divisional Artillery C/186 moved to rest at HOUTKERQUE with 174th Brigade, R.F.A.	Appendix 2 reference Sheet 27 and 28 1/40000
"	10/4/17		Left Group 39th Divisional Artillery re-inforced by B/104 (18 pdrs) and one section Howitzers from D/104.	
"	10/4/17		Left Group became M.Group. Copy of locations of units of 39th Divisional Artillery attached numbered Appendix 2.	
"	11/4/17		B/186 One gunner wounded.	
"	13/4/17		B/186 One driver wounded.	
"	16/4/17	7.30AM	39th Divisional Infantry relieved by 33rd Division. and K.Group came under the orders of that Division.	
"	20/4/17	11-30pm	186th Brigade, R.F.A. relieved in the line by 189 Artillery Brigade and moved to rest billets at HERZEELE.	
HERZEELE	21/4/17		186th Brigade, R.F.A. carried out battery training.	
	25/4/17		B/186 moved into action to re-inforce 58th Divisional Artillery.	
	26/4/17		A/186 " " " " " " "	
	29/4/17		2/Lieut R.A.Young granted 10 weeks leave to South Africa and struck off the strength.	

Charles Lee
Comdg 186 Bde R.F.A.

S E C R E T

39th Divisional Artillery

Ref: 1/40h000 Sheets 27 and 28   LOCATIONS   10th April, 1917

Unit	Group	Gun Position	Wagon Lines	Remarks
H.Q.R.A.	–	28 G.34.b.2.2.	–	RENINGHELST
H.Q. 174 Bde	–	HOUTKERQUE	27 E.14.d.	)
A.Batty	–	–	27 E.13.d.9.3.	)
B.Batty	–	–	27 K.5.a.6.4	) Corps
C.Batty	–	–	27 K.5.c.2.8	) Reserve
D.Batty	–	–	27 H.7.b.2.5	)
H.Q. 186 Bde	Left	28 I.14.b.1.8	28. H.7.b.2.5.	
A.Batty	"	28 I.8.d.30.45	28 G.10.a.9.0	
B.Batty	"	28 I.8.d.3.7	(28 G.9.b.1.8	
C.Batty (4)	"	–	(28 G.9.b.6.3. 27 D.10.b.2.5	Cps Reserve
C.Batty (2)	Left	28 I.3.d.65.55	28 H.13.c.4.6	
D.Batty	"	28 I.8.c.8.3	28 H.7.b.2.5.	
B/104 A.F.A. Bde (4)	"	28 I.27.b.2.8)		
" (2)	"	28 I.27.b.5.3)	28 G.23.c.5.3.	
D/104 A.F.A. Bde (2)	"	28 I.8.c.8.3	28 G.28.b.5.4	
H.Q.D.A.C.	–	Place Berthin, POPERINGHE.		
No.1 Sec.	–	–	28 G.19.b.9.8	
No.2 Sec	–	–	28 G.15.c.5.5	
No.3 Sec	–	–	27 D.8.c.8.6.	Corps Reserve
H.Q.T.M.Batts)				
V.Batty)				
X.Batty)	–	27 D.8.c.8.6		Corps Reserve
Z.Batty)				
Y.Batty	)H.Q.23rd T.M.Btts.	28 H.13.d.9.3.		Attached 23rd T.m. Batts.

9/4/17   s/1 Brigade Major, R.A.,

Army Form C. 2118

WAR DIARY
or
INTELLIGENCE SUMMARY

(Erase heading not required.)

Sheet 6
Volume II.

Last appendix 2
186th Brigade, R.F.A.

Instructions regarding War Diaries and Intelligence Summaries are contained in F.S. Regs., Part II. and the Staff Manual respectively. Title Pages. will be prepared in manuscript.

Place	Date	Hour	Summary of Events and Information	Remarks and references to Appendices
HERZEELE	3.5.17	9 a.m.	The 186th Brigade, R.F.A., commenced to march to training ground at POLINCOVE arriving in NOORDPEENE at 2 p.m. and went into billets for the night.	Ref. Sheet 28 France.
NOORDPEENE	4.5	8 a.m.	Continued the march arriving at POLINCOVE at 2 p.m.	
POLINCOVE	5.5		Training Commenced on training area at NORTLEULINGHEM	
"	16.5		Training finished.	
"	17.5	8.30 a.m.	The Brigade marched to RUBROUCK arriving at 2 p.m.	
RUBROUCK	18.5	8.30 a.m.	The Brigade marched to HERZEELE arriving at 12 noon and went into billets.	
HERZEELE	20/21		B. & C/186 went into action relieving A. & C/298 in the following positions C/186 I.2.c.75.55 and came under orders of R.Group 39th D.A. B/186 I.2.a.05.50 Z4 guns) and C.26.d.7.1 (2 guns) and came under the orders of Left Group 55th Div. Artillery. The 55th Division being on the Right and the 38th Division on the left.	
"	23.5		A/186 marched into the forward area and proceeded to prepare a new position at I.1.b.35.70.	
"	26.5		H.Q. 186th Brigade, R.F.A. moved into Reigersburg with wagon lines at A.19.d.2.2. D/186 moving to wagon lines of R.Group 39th Div. Artillery. Lt-Colonel C.H. Kilner assumed command of R.Group 39th Div. Artillery.	
REIGERSBURG	28.5		D/186 brought one section of guns into action at I.1.b.60.20	
"	"		A/186 " two " " " " " I.1.b.35.70.	

O.C. 186ᵗʰ Bde R.F.A

Army Form C. 2118

Instructions regarding War Diaries and Intelligence Summaries are contained in F.S. Regs., Part II. and the Staff Manual respectively. Title Pages will be prepared in manuscript.

WAR DIARY or INTELLIGENCE SUMMARY
(Erase heading not required.)

Sheet 7
Volume 2.

186 Brigade RFA

Place	Date	Hour	Summary of Events and Information	Remarks and references to Appendices
Reigersburg.	1/6/17		A/186 brought remaining section into action at I.1.b.35.70, the whole position being changed to I.1.b.35.70.	
	1/6/17		B/186 brought remaining two sections into action at I.1.b.60.50.	
	1/6/17 to 7/6/17		The artillery of this Group carried out counter battery work and kept up a harassing fire on the enemy's communications both by day and night to assist the contemplated offensive by the Xth, IXth and 2nd Anzac Corps on our right. On the 3rd, 5th and 6th June, practice barrages were put down on the enemy's lines in front of WIELTJE, enemy's reply rather weak. Gas was discharged into the enemys lines during the nights of 5/6th 6/7th, and our howitzers fired gas shells against known battery positions during the nights 4/5th 5/6th 6/7th. At 3.10 a.m. to 3.30 a.m. 7/6/17 our artillery made a demonstration to assist the Xth Corps whose attack on Mount SORREL and HILL 60 was launched at that hour, and afterwards engaged in counter battery work with aeroplane observation. The enemy's reply was weak and consisted mainly of a few gas shells on battery positions. C/186 was heavily shelled with 5.9's and 4.2's on the 3rd, 4th and 6th, very little damage done except to the ammunition dump which was blown up on the third.	
	8/6/17	1.30 7.30	C/186 was again heavily shelled with projectiles of all calibres up to 8", two gun pits were hit and set on fire, this battery moved to a new position on the 9th. The following casualties were sustained.	
	7/6/17		B/186 Major G.C.Kemp wounded (Gassed) C/186 Three O.R's wounded. D/186 One O.R. killed and two O.R's wounded.	Appendix No. 3 Casualties
	8/6/17		D/186 Two other Ranks killed. C/186 One O.R.Killed and two O.R's wounded.	

Army Form C. 2118

WAR DIARY
or
INTELLIGENCE SUMMARY 186th Brigade, R.F.A.

Last appendix 2
Sheet 6
Volume II.

(Erase heading not required.)

Instructions regarding War Diaries and Intelligence Summaries are contained in F.S. Regs., Part II. and the Staff Manual respectively. Title Pages, will be prepared in manuscript.

Place	Date	Hour	Summary of Events and Information	Remarks and references to Appendices
HERZEELE	3.5.17	9a.m.	The 186th Brigade, R.F.A., commenced to march to training ground at POLINCOVE arriving in NOORDPEENE at 2 p.m. and went into billets for the night.	
NOORDPEENE	4.5	8a.m.	Continued the march arriving at POLINCOVE at 2 p.m.	
POLINCOVE	5.5		Training Commenced on training area at NORTLEULINGHEM	
"	16.5		Training finished.	
"	17.5	8.30a.m	The Brigade marched to RUBROUCK arriving at 2 p.m.	
RUBROUCK	18.5	8.30a.m	The Brigade marched to HERZEELE arriving at 12 noon and went into billets.	
HERZEELE	20/21		B.& C/186 went into action relieving A. & C/298 in the following positions C/186 I.2.c.75.55 and came under orders of R.Group 39th D.A. B/186 I.2.a.05.50 Z4 guns) and C.26.d.7.1 (2 guns) and came under the orders of Left Group 55th Div.Artillery. The 55th Division being on the Right and the 38th Division on the left.	Ref. Sheet 28 France.
"	23.5		A/186 marched into the forward area and proceeded to prepare a new position at I.1.b.35.70.	
"	26.5		H.Q.186th Brigade, R.F.A. moved into Reigersburg with wagon lines at A.19.d.2.2. D/186 moving to wagon lines at L.3.b.4.6. Sheet 27. Lt-Colonel C.H.Kilner assumed command of R.Group 39th Div.Artillery.	
REIGERSBURG	28.5		D/186 brought one section of guns into action at I.1.b.60.20	
"	"		A/186 " two " " " " " I.1.b.35.70.	

CMKilner
Lt.Col.
O.C. 186th Bde R.F.A.

Army Form C. 2118

WAR DIARY or INTELLIGENCE SUMMARY

Sheet 7
Volume 2.

(Erase heading not required.)

186 Bryan RFA

Place	Date	Hour	Summary of Events and Information	Remarks and references to Appendices
Reigersburg.	1/6/17		A/186 brought remaining section into action at I.1.b.35.70, the whole position being changed to I.1.b.35.70.	
	1/6/17		B/186 brought remaining two sections into action at I.1.b.60.50.	
	1/6/17 to 7/6/17		The artillery of this Group carried out counter battery work and kept up a harassing fire on the enemy's communications both by day and night to assist the contemplated offensive by the Xth, IXth and 2nd Anzac Corps on our right. On the 3rd, 5th and 6th June, practice barrages were put down on the enemy's lines in front of WIELTJE, enemy's reply rather weak. Gas was discharged into the enemys lines during the nights of 5/6th 6/7th, and our howitzers fired gas shells against known battery positions during the nights 4/5th 5/6th 6/7th. At 3.10 a.m. to 3.30 a.m. 7/6/17 our artillery made a demonstration to assist the Xth Corps whose attack on Mount SORREL and HILL 60 was launched at that hour, and afterwards engaged in counter battery work with aeroplane observation. and a large number of hostile batteries being engaged and silenced. The enemy's reply was weak and consisted mainly of a few gas shells on battery positions. C/186 was heavily shelled with 5.9's and 4.2's on the 3rd, 4th and 6th, very little damage done except to the ammunition dump which was blown up on the third.	
	8/6/17	1.30 7.30	C/186 was again heavily shelled with projectiles of all calibres up to 8", two gun pits were hit and set on fire, this battery moved to a new position on the 9th. The following casualties were sustained.	
	7/6/17		B/186 Major G.C. Kemp Wounded (Gassed) C/186 Three O.R's wounded. D/186 One O.R. Killed and two O.R's wounded.	Appendix No. 3 Casualties
	8/6/17		D/186 Two other Ranks killed. C/186 One O.R. Killed and two O.R's wounded.	

Army Form C. 2118

WAR DIARY
or
INTELLIGENCE SUMMARY 186th Brigade, R.F.A.

Last appendix 2
Sheet 6
Volume II.

(Erase heading not required.)

Instructions regarding War Diaries and Intelligence Summaries are contained in F.S. Regs., Part II. and the Staff Manual respectively. Title Pages. will be prepared in manuscript.

Place	Date	Hour	Summary of Events and Information	Remarks and references to Appendices
HERZEELE	3.5.17	9 a.m.	The 186th Brigade, R.F.A., commenced to march to training ground at POLINCOVE arriving in NOORDPEENE at 2 p.m. and went into billets for the night.	Ref. Sheet 28 France.
NOORDPEENE	4.5	8 a.m.	Continued the march arriving at POLINCOVE at 2 p.m.	
POLINCOVE	5.5		Training Commenced on training area at NORTLEULINGHEM	
"	16.5		Training finished.	
"	17.5	8.30 a.m.	The Brigade marched to RUBROUCK arriving at 2 p.m.	
RUBROUCK	18.5	8.30 a.m.	The Brigade marched to HERZEELE arriving at 12 noon and went into billets.	
HERZEELE	20/21		B.& C/186 went into action relieving A. & C/298 in the following positions C/186 I.2.c.75.55 and came under orders of R.Group 39th D.A. B/186 I.2.a.05.50 Z4 guns) and C.26.d.7.1 (2 guns) and came under the orders of Left Group 55th Div.Artillery. The 55th Division being on the Right and the 38th Division on the left.	
"	23.5		A/186 marched into the forward area and proceeded to prepare a new position at I.1.b.35.70.	
"	26.5		H.Q.186th Brigade, R.F.A. moved into Reigersburg with wagon lines at A.19.d.2.2. D/186 moving to wagon lines at L.3.b.4.6. Sheet 27. Lt-Colonel C.H.Kilner assumed command of R.Group 39th Div.Artillery.	
REIGERSBURG	28.5		D/186 brought one section of guns into action at I.1.b.60.30	
"	"		A/186 " two " " " " " " I.1.b.35.70.	

C.H.Kilner Lt.Col.
O.C. 186 Bde R.F.A.

Army Form C. 2118

WAR DIARY
or
INTELLIGENCE SUMMARY
(Erase heading not required.)

Sheet 7 Volume 2.

182 Bryn RFA

Place	Date	Hour	Summary of Events and Information	Remarks and references to Appendices
Reigersburg.	1/6/17		A/186 brought remaining section into action at I.1.b.35.70, the whole position being changed to I.1.b.35.70.	
	1/6/17		D/186 brought remaining two sections into action at I.1.b.60.50.	
	1/6/17 to 7/6/17		The artillery of this Group carried out counter battery work and kept up a harassing fire on the enemy's communications both by day and night to assist the contemplated offensive by the Xth, IXth and 2nd Anzac Corps on our right. On the 3rd, 5th and 6th June, practice barrages were put down on the enemy's lines in front of WIELTJE, enemy's reply rather weak. Gas was discharged into the enemy's lines during the nights of 5/6th 6/7th, and our howitzers fired gas shells against known battery positions during the nights 4/5th 5/6th 6/7th. At 3.10 a.m. to 3.30 a.m. 7/6/17 our artillery made a demonstration to assist the Xth Corps whose attack on Mount SORREL and HILL 60 was launched at that hour, and afterwards engaged in counter battery work with aeroplane observation. and a large number of hostile batteries being engaged and silenced. The enemy's reply was weak and consisted mainly of a few gas shells on battery positions. C/186 was heavily shelled with 5.9's and 4.2's on the 3rd, 4th and 6th, very little damage done except to the ammunition dump which was blown up on the third.	
	8/6/17 1.30 7.30		C/186 was again heavily shelled with projectiles of all calibres up to 8", two gun pits were hit and set on fire, this battery moved to a new position on the 9th. The following were sustained.	Appendix No.3 Casualties
	7/6/17		B/186 Major G.C.Kemp Wounded (Gassed) C/186 Three O.R's wounded. D/186 One O.R. killed and two O.R's wounded.	
	8/6/17		D/186 Two other Ranks killed. C/186 One O.R.Killed and two O.R's wounded.	

Army Form C. 2118

WAR DIARY
or
INTELLIGENCE SUMMARY — 186 Brigade R.F.A

Sheet 8
Volume 2.

(Erase heading not required.)

Place	Date	Hour	Summary of Events and Information	Remarks and references to Appendices
				Appendix No. 4. Honours and Awards.
	10/6/17		The following officers were posted as shown and are struck off. 2/Lt.S.E.Lamb Transferred to R.F.C. 24/5/17. 2/Lt.A.Wale " 39th D.A.C. 24/5/17. 2/Lt.A.S.Barnes " R.F.C. 1/6/17.	
	11/6/17		The following Officers joined and are posted as shown. 2/Lt.H.B.Compton to A/186 24/5/17 2/Lt.W.H.G.Compton " B/186 24/5/17.	
	13/6/17		D/186 Four other ranks wounded, two of these died in hospital next day.	
	16/6/17		D/186 One O.R. wounded	
	17/6/17		C/186 One O.R. wounded.	
	19/6/17		B/186 One O.R. killed and three O.R's wounded. C/186 Four O.R's wounded. B/186 2/Lieut W.H.G.Compton Killed. B/186 One O.R. killed and two O.R's wounded.	
			During the period 7/6/17 to 22/6/17 many batteries of this division were heavily shelled and many casualties sustained. The enemy also shelled all roads and tracks and caused considerable casualties to ammunition and supply wagons. Brigade H.Q. was shelled on the 18th and one O.R. was killed and five wounded, these belonged to Signal personnel attached.	
	22/6/17		B/186 withdrawn from line to rest.	
	24/6/17		39th Divisional Artillery re-organised into two groups, the Right Group at Reigersburg being under the command of Lt-Colonel C.H.Kilner, and consists of the following batteries, A/186, D/186 and C/174, A/174 leaving their guns in position to answer call for S.O.S, C/186, B/174 and D/174 being withdrawn to rest.	

Army Form C. 2118

WAR DIARY
or
INTELLIGENCE SUMMARY

(Erase heading not required.)

186 Brigade RFA

Sheet 9
Volume 2.

Place	Date	Hour	Summary of Events and Information	Remarks and references to Appendices
	25/6/17		The Left Group at TROIS TOURS under Colonel Archdale consist of A/77, C/77 and D/77 Army Field Artillery Brigade.	
	26/6/17		A/186 One O.R. wounded. A/186 Major E.C.R.Kilkelly killed by Shell Fire.	
	27/6/17		D/186 One O.R. wounded. A/186 One O.R. killed and Three O.R's wounded.	
	28/29/6/17		During the night 28/29th the vicinity of Reigersburg (Group H.Q) was heavily shelled with 15 and 10.5 c.m. Hows about 400 rounds being fired, the Chateau was hit but no casualties sustained.	

CASUALTIES

76125	Gnr. Satchell F.	Wounded at duty	31/5/17	D/186
	Major G.C. Kemp	Gassed - in hospital	7/6/17	B/186
31356	Gnr. Locke C.	Wounded - in hospital	7/6/17	C/186
L/1901	" Smith P.	Wounded at duty	"	"
L/1893	" Wright W.R.	" "	"	"
47692	Gnr. Heard H.	Killed	7/6/17	D/186
13478	Gnr. Nicholson E.	Wounded - in hospital	"	D/186
34017	Gnr. Hill S.E.	" "	"	"
121240	Cpl. Mustoe H.	Killed	8/6/17	"
41688	Gnr. Crosby W.	Killed	"	"
38435	Gnr. Elliot S.F.	Killed	"	C/186
1919	Cpl. Strachan F.	Wounded - at duty	"	"
38311	Gnr. Dixon A.G.	" "	"	"
41641	A/Bdr. Keech A.J.	Wounded and gassed(died)	10/6/17	D/186
28585	Gnr. Lewington S.	" " " "	"	"
26812	Gnr Wood P.	" " "	"	"
152835	Gnr. Perry W.T.	" " "	"	"
47684	Gnr. Roddis F.	Gassed	11/6/17	"
38366	Bdr. Crawshay H.C.	Wounded - at duty	"	C/186
38128	Gnr. Parish J.H.	Killed	13/6/17	B/186
31936	Cpl. Priestly A.R.	Wounded	"	"
38181	Gnr. Chambers H.	Gassed	"	"
38084	S.S. Nagle E.	Wounded	"	"
122382	A/Bdr. Lewis V.J.	Wounded - in hospital	16/6/17	C/186
38400	Gnr. Kirkbride A.	" "	"	"
40229	Gnr. Simpson C.A.	Wounded - at duty	"	"
40140	Bdr. Pritchard P.	" "	"	"
	2/Lieut W.H.G. Compton	Killed	17/6/17	B/186
152367	Gnr. Sollitt H.	Wounded - in hospital	19/6/17	"
635577	Gnr. White D.	Injured	"	"
86164	Gnr. Newton F.C.	Killed	"	"
174179	Gnr. Storer F.	Wounded - in hospital	"	D/186
47511	Bdr. Connelly J.	Wounded - at duty	25/6/17	A/186
	Major E.C.R. Kilkelly	Killed	26/6/16	A/186
81360	Gnr. Danby G.	Wounded - at duty	"	D/186
111910	Gnr. Butler G.	Killed	27/6/17	A/186
26745	Gnr. Letton R.	Wounded - in hospital	"	"
32681	Gnr. Waller	" "	"	"
152209	Gnr. Lawton F.	Wounded - at duty	"	"
	2/Lieut R.J. Slatter	Wounded - in hospital	28/6/17	B/186
36493	Bdr. Kilshaw E.	Wounded - in hospital	"	"

Lieut & Adjt.,

186th Brigade, R.F.A.,

Army Form C. 2118.

Instructions regarding War Diaries and Intelligence Summaries are contained in F. S. Regs., Part II. and the Staff Manual respectively. Title pages will be prepared in manuscript.

WAR DIARY Last appendix 9.
or
INTELLIGENCE SUMMARY. 186th Brigade, R.F.A.

Last sheet 16. Sheet 17 Volume 2.

(Erase heading not required.)

Place	Date	Hour	Summary of Events and Information	Remarks and references to Appendices
Lock 7.	1.10.17.		Harassing fire going on night and day. 2 Army Barrages 9.30 a.m. & 8.15 p.m.	Honours & Rewards
			The positions occupied by 186th Bde R.F.A. heavily shelled for the greater part of the day.	Appendix 10
			2/Lieuts G.A.Wilson and J.A.W.Griffiths wounded 2 O.R's killed and 12 O.R's wounded.	
	2.10.17.		Major G.I.Thomas and 2/Lieut W.Patchett wounded.	
			2/Lt C.P.Howard joined and posted to D/186	
	3.10.17.		Three O.R's wounded.	Casualties
	4.10.17.		The 2nd Army attacked over a wide front at 6 a.m. and secured most of their objectives which included the main ridge at Broodseinde. The objectives on the zone covered by the 39th Divisional Artillery were limited to the capture of a few strong points which included Berry Cotts	Appendix 11
			these they failed to secure owing to intense M.G.fire from Kamp Farm, and artillery fire from the Tenbrielen Group.	
			One O.R. wounded.	
			Harassing fire continued day and night and army barrages fired at intervals.	
	6.10.17.		2/Lieut J.E.Warner wounded at duty, three O.R's wounded.	
			Major F.E.Spencer wounded.	
	7.10.17.		The 186th Brigade, R.F.A. relieved by 123rd Brigade R.F.A. 37th Division.	
			and moved to rest Billets at Strazeele.	
	8./25/10/17.		186th Brigade R.F.A. resting and refitting.	
	26.10.17		Moved to Curragh and Swift Camps M.17.c.4.7 Sheet 28	
	8.10.17		Capt S.I.Quin appointed A/Major and posted to A/186	
	9.10.17		A/Major F.Barry and A/Capt W.B.Carter joined and posted to C/186 & B/186 respectively.	
	15.10.17		2/Lieut E.V.Mason and 2/Lieut H.B.S.Hodlinott joined and posted to A/186 & D/186 respectively.	

Army Form C. 2118.

WAR DIARY
or
INTELLIGENCE SUMMARY. 186 Brigade RFA

SHEET 10   Last appendix 9.
Volume 2.

(Erase heading not required.)

Place	Date	Hour	Summary of Events and Information	Remarks and references to Appendices
	25.10.17.		2/Lieut A.McNab joined and posted to B/186	
			" J.A.Wilcock " " " D/186	
			" G.H.Bartram " " " C/186	
			" W.H.Freeston " " " B/186	
	25.10.17.		2/Lieut B.O.E.Walpole. posted to 39th D.A.C.	

C.W.Kitson LtCol
Comdg 186ᵗʰ Bde RFA

Appendix 11

CASUALTIES

1st Oct.	61736 Bdr. Paine W.R.	Wounded at duty	A/186
	31898 Sgt. Hughes W.E.	Wounded	B/186
	2/Lieut G.A. Wilson	"	D/186
	" J.A.W. Griffith	"	"
	100664 Gnr. Wright S.W.	Killed	"
	2742 B.Q.M.S. Froud	Wounded	"
	147054 Cpl. Witney G	"	"
	41662 Gnr. Rennie C.	"	"
	226022 Gnr. Myall W.	"	"
	72308 Gnr. Hake S.	"	"
	38363 Gnr. Ashmore W.E.	Killed	C/186
	731105 Gnr. Levi B.	Wounded	"
	38369 Bdr. Lang G.	"	"
	665063 Gnr. Mitchell J.	"	"
	416634 Gnr. Sheldrick	"	A/186
2nd Oct.	Major G.I. Thomas D.S.O., M.C.,	Wounded	A/186
	2/Lieut W. Patchett	"	"
3rd Oct	755573 A/Bdr. Thomas J.	Wounded	D/186
	41748 Cpl. Beach W.	"	"
	10055 Sgt. Bell G.	Wounded at duty	"
6th Oct	2/Lieut J.E. Warner	Wounded at duty	A/186
	41754 Gnr. Costello J.J.	Wounded	D/186
	2742 B.Q.M.S. Froud	"	"
7th Oct	Major F.E. Spencer M.C.	Wounded	C/186

HONOURS AND AWARDS

Appendix 10

111171 Bdr. G.W. Drew	Military Medal	D/186
Major G. Heron M.C.	*Second* Bar to Military Cross	D/186
2742 B.Q.M.S. Froud	Distinguished Conduct Medal	D/186
33549 Cpl. G.W. Harris	Military Medal	A/186
32686 A/Bdr. J.H. Cockrell	"	A/186

31 x 17

Hill Capt & adjt
186 Bde RFA

Army Form C. 2118.

(Last Sheet 18) Sheet 19 **WAR DIARY** 186 Bryade RFA
Volume II.   Last appendix 11.

or

INTELLIGENCE SUMMARY.

(Erase heading not required.)

Place	Date	Hour	Summary of Events and Information	Remarks and references to Appendices
Manor Farm	1/11/17	3 p.m.	The 186th Brigade, R.F.A. relieved the 18th Brigade A.R.F.A. at 3 p.m. with H.Qrs and battery positions as follows:-	Casualties Appendix 12.
			Lt-Col.C.H.Kilner assumed command of A.Group	
			A/186 I.29.c.9.7	
			B/186 I.28.c.85.40	
			C/186 I.28.b.28.47	
			D/186 I.28.d.19.77	
			45th Australian Battery I.29.b.85.39	
"	2/11/17	5.55 am	Fired on Army Barrage.	
"	4/11/17	4.40 am	Fired an Army Barrage.	
"	5/11/17	4.0 am	Fired a barrage to cover operations by 50th Division against dug-outs at J.21.d.8.8, the Infantry were held up by uncut wire and failed to secure their objective.	
"	"	4.50 am	Fired an Army Barrage.	
"	6/11/17	6 a.m.	Fired a barrage to cover operations against Pollerhoek Chateau.	
"	1 to 9/11/17		Harassing fire carried out every night on enemy communications.	
"	"	2 p.m.	D/186 relieved by D/189 and withdrew to wagon lines.	
"	11/11/17	10 am	A/186 relieved by A/174 " "	
"	12/11/17		D/186 moved into position at J.13.c.17.33	
"	13/11/17		A/186 " " " I.24.b.83.67	
"	"	7 am.	C/186 " " " J.13.c.27.60	
"	14/11/17		B/186 moved one Section to I.24.a.75.30	
"	15/11/17	10 a.m.	B/186 " two Sections to I.24.a.75.30	
			The 186th Brigade, R. F. A forming part of the Northern Group 39th Divl Artillery, came under the orders of Lt-Col J. Allardyce and the H.Qrs 186th Brigade, R.F.A. withdrew to Wagon Lines at CURRAGH CAMP.	
	17/11/17		Major S.I.Quin wounded gassed	
	18/11/17		The 186th Brigade R.F.A. withdrew to wagon lines being relieved by 149th Brigade, R. F. A 30th Division.	

Army Form C. 2118.

WAR DIARY
or
INTELLIGENCE—SUMMARY. 186th Bde R.F.A.

Sheet 20 Volume 11.

(Erase heading not required.)

Place	Date	Hour	Summary of Events and Information	Remarks and references to Appendices
	10/11/17		Major P. Wright) Mounted Gassed. 2/Lieut R.A.Young) " A. McNab) " J.E. Darner)	
	23/11/17		The 39th Division transferred to the VIIIth Corps. The 186th Brigade R.F.A. marched to wagon lines near VLAMERTINGHE 28 H.9.d. the officers and other ranks suffering from the effects of gas were sent to WATOU for a period of rest.	
	25/11/17		Lt-Col.C.H.Kilner posted to England.	

- CASUALTIES -

Date	Number & Name	Status	Unit
4/11/17	38315 Sgt. Willis	Wounded	C/186
5/11/17	68013 Sgt. Batt H.	Wounded Gassed	A/186
6/11/17	1027 S.Sgt Roberts A.O.C.	Wounded	H.Q/186
7/11/17	152209 Gnr. Lawton F.	Wounded gassed	A/186
8/11/17	26711 Gnr. Burton E.	"	"
9/11/17	22573 A/Bdr Dye J	"	"
10/11/17	205334 Gnr. Marshall	"	"
11/11/17	31981 Gnr. Angus W.	"	"
12/11/17	62216 Sgt. Jones W.	"	"
	214523 Gnr. Fuller R	"	"
14/11/17	210323 Gnr. Pedley W.	"	"
15/11/17	41767 Gnr. Matthews S.		"
16/11/17	186986 Gnr. Course J.	Wounded	"
17/11/17	31988 A/Bdr. Delieu T.	Wounded gassed	"
	31883 Gnr. Fells A.J.	"	"
	Major S.I. Quin	"	"
18/11/17	66023 Gnr. Mosscrop J.	"	"
	2322 Gnr. Hall H.H.	"	"
	825777 Gnr. Clarke G.	"	"
	159734 Gnr. Harris H.	"	C/186
	161101 Gnr. Haylock T.	"	"
	97022 Gnr. Hunt J.	"	"
	22124 Gnr. Kirkhope G.	"	"
	38430 Bdr. Odlin J.	"	"
	38458 Gnr. Ecroyd W.	"	"
	961432 Gnr. Lindon J.W.	"	"
	97068 Gnr. Coffey T.	"	"
	38473 Sgt. Monteith J.B.	"	"
	40141 Cpl. Pritchard P.	"	"
	117302 Bdr. Allen W.	"	"
	42265 Gnr. Evans G.H.	"	"
	17543 Gnr. McMillan D.	"	"
	193381 Gnr. Coulson D.	"	"
	Major. P. Wright	"	B/186
	2/Lieut R.A. Young	"	"
	" A. McNab	"	"
	" J.E. Warner	"	A/186
19/11/17	32686 A/Bdr. Cockle E.J.	"	"
	65035 Sgt. Bilton J.E.	"	"
	31875 Sgt. Dixon A.	"	"
	26684 Cpl. Hicks A.E.	"	"
	28237 Bdr. Gummer H.J.C.	"	"
	26750 Bdr. Nicholson A.J.	"	"
	61736 Gnr. Payne W.R.	"	"
	31941 Gnr. Regan J.	"	"
	12019 Gnr. Froggett E.	"	"
	5262 Sgt. Powery W.	"	D/186
	35960 Cpl. Ward A.	"	"
	65993 Gnr. Chapman G.	"	"
	122565 Gnr. Rumbles A.J.	"	"
	28563 Gnr. Knott C.	"	"
	41649 Gnr. Smith A.C.	"	"
	41612 Dr. Vincent J.	"	"
20/11/17	84808 Sgt. Davis L.A.	"	A/186
	19742 Bdr. Kipling W.	"	"
	26735 Gnr. Bishop W.	"	"
	26778 Gnr. Dixon W.	"	"

20/11/17	38164	Sgt.Smith J.P.	Wounded gassed	B/186
	94069	Bdr.Walker P.	"	"
	25441	Cpl.Williams P.	"	"
	31867	Bdr.Cowley W.F.	"	"
	227195	Gnr.McCreadie J.	"	"
	152361	Gnr.Harrison W.	"	"
	218246	Gnr.McNichol J.	"	"
	227765	Gnr.McEwan J.B.	"	"
	150525	Gnr.Grimmett A.J.	"	"
	23751	Gnr.Martin A.S.	"	"
	955094	Cpl.Stafford W.M.	"	"
	31892	Bdr.Gregory T.H.	"	"
	171263	Gnr.Nield S.	"	"
	1927	Gnr.Whelan J.	"	"
	144945	Gnr.Geldard E	"	"
	185912	Gnr.Osborne H.	"	"
	38179	Gnr.Green H.J.	"	"
	13721	Gnr.Preston H.	"	"
	935711	Gnr.Eastick C.	"	C/186
	93197	Gnr.Whitehead	"	"
	92679	Bdr.Holland A.	"	"
	149356	Gnr.Hexter A.E.	"	"
	152406	Gnr.Marsden	"	"
	40117	Sgt.Adams C.	"	"
24/11/17	1898	Gnr.Newton W.	"	B/186
	218177	Gnr.Mitchell H.	"	"
	26725	Gnr.Bishop W.H.	"	A/186
30/11/17		Sap.Milton R.	Wounded	39th D.Sigs attached H.Q 186.
	312107	Sap.Bolton H.R.	"	

Casualties   Appendix 13

Date	Number	Rank	Name	Status	Unit
3/12/17	30881	Bdr	Terry E	Wounded	D/186
	72463	"	Still AJ	Shell Shock	"
	40784	Gnr	Ince H	—	"
	41565	Dr	Wyatt CE	—	"
5/12/17	41271	Gnr	Hood A	Killed	HQ/186
	41796	Dr	Edmonds HG	—	"
	26863	Gnr	Lovett J	—	"
	36285	Cpl	Cole A	Wounded	"
	904	Gnr	Veasey FJ	—	"
	31922	Gnr	Lock J	Killed	B/186
	3915	Dr	Walsh J	Wounded	"
	38189	"	Robson RA	—	"
	31882	"	Edgeley E	—	"
	176719	Gnr	Rymer W	—	"
	225097	Dr	Rumans C	—	"
		Capt AE Delgado RAMC		—	HQ/186
		Capt V Hill		Wounded at duty	"
		Capt WB Carter		—	B/186
		Lieut Donk Johnston		Wounded	D/186
9/12/17		Capt V Hawkins		—	A/186
	31938	Sgt	Pitt CE	—	"
	42124	Cpl	Hancock JL	—	"
	40609	Bdr	Monks EL	—	"
14/12/17	117246	Bdr	Munby ES	Killed	C/186
	1901	Gnr	Smith P	Wounded	"
15/12/17	41594	Cpl Wh	Miles JL	—	D/186
	751894	Gnr	Logan J	—	"
	222500	"	Lloyd G	—	"
	238313	"	Burden SB	—	"
	238403	"	Chant J	—	"
	238417	"	Banford SE	—	"
	237213	"	Smith J	—	"
	165285	"	Pike EA	—	"
	12240	"	Harrison GH	—	"
17/12/17	41760	Gnr	Webb WJ	—	
20/12/17	41907	Bdr	Martin	—	A/186
	32656	Dr	Buss AB	—	"
	32664	g/s	Stacey AH	—	"
	676664	Gnr	Vaughan J	—	"
	38182	"	Robinson C	—	D/186

(Last Sheet 20) Sheet 21   Last Appendix 12   Army Form C. 2118.

WAR DIARY
or
INTELLIGENCE SUMMARY.
(Erase heading not required.)

Volume II   186 Brigade R.F.A.

Vol 22

Place	Date	Hour	Summary of Events and Information	Remarks and references to Appendices
	18.11.17		Major N.S. Nicholson joined from the BMSE and posted to A/1/86	Appendix
			Capt E.N. Clarke appointed Acting Major and posted to B/1/86	13
			2/Lt V.C. Hawkins — " — Captain and 2nd in Command of A/1/86	
VLAMERTINGHE	21.11.17		2/Lieuts H.E. Scarlys and L.S. Locker joined and posted to A & B/1/86 respectively	
	22.11.17		Lieut Col L.J. Henderson posted to Command 186 Bde R.F.A. vice Lieut Colonel Kelve, to England	
	5.12.17		Lieut Col Lord R.E. Norman posted to Command 186 Bde R.F.A vice Lieut Colonel L.J. Henderson posted to 45th Brigade R.F.A	
			The following officers joined and were posted to batteries as stated :-	
			2/Lt N. Ledlie A/186 2/Lt W. Garbutt A/186 2/Lt D.J. Fitzgerald B/186 2/Lt J.C. Gibbon C/186	
			Brigade H.Q. were bombed with a bomb dropped from an enemy aeroplane Capt Carlos R.F.A. Capt delegate R.A.M.C. Capt V. Pree Adjt 1/86, Lieut Smith Johnston, B/186 being wounded at duty. Three men Hdqrs Staff being killed and one wounded. One man B/186 killed and five men wounded.	
	28.B.25.a.95.d.9.12.17		Hdqrs 186 Bde R.F.A moved into action and Lt-Col R.E. Norman took command of N°2 Group, 33rd Divl Artillery with Hdqrs at LOW FARM D.25.a.95.45 Sh 28	
Low Farm				

Army Form C. 2118.

Sheet 22
Volume II

WAR DIARY
or
INTELLIGENCE SUMMARY. 186 Brigade RFA

(Erase heading not required.)

Instructions regarding War Diaries and Intelligence Summaries are contained in F. S. Regs., Part II. and the Staff Manual respectively. Title pages will be prepared in manuscript.

Place	Date	Hour	Summary of Events and Information	Remarks and references to Appendices
LOMPRET	7/9/17		A/D/186 moved into the line at the same time with positions at D.15.d.47.77 and D.14.a.80.35 relieving two Batteries of the 158 Brigade RFA. No 2 Group consisted of 4 batteries A+D/186 and B+C/158	
	9.12.17	12.50am	German wireless message intercepted which pointed to a German attack on the Passchendaele front at about 6am. but this did not develop	
	12-12-17	12 noon	B+C/186 came into action and relieved B+C/158 with positions at B.16.a.23.73 and D.15.d.92.92 respectively.	
	12.12.17		Grouping of Artillery reorganized, No 2 Group under the command of Lt Colonel Lord A L Browne consisting of the following batteries:—	
			A/186 in position at D.15.d.47.77	
			B/186 —"— D.16.a.23.73	
			C/186 —"— D.15.d.32.92	
			D/186 —"— D.15.b.90.30	
			B/162 —"— B.16.c.97.95	
			C/162 —"— D.16.a.40.35	
			D/162 —"— D.9.c.68.12	

Sheet 23

WAR DIARY
or
INTELLIGENCE SUMMARY.   186 Brigade R.F.A.

Volume II

(Erase heading not required.)

Army Form C. 2118.

Place	Date	Hour	Summary of Events and Information	Remarks and references to Appendices
LA PANNE	20		The 162 Brigade R.F.A. withdrew to Wagon lines	
	21		The 186 Brigade R.F.A. were relieved by 251 Brigade R.F.A. and withdrew to Wagon lines at MAMERTINGHE.	
MAMERTINGHE	22		The 186 Brigade R.F.A. moved to Wagon lines at H.5.d. Brigade HQrs being established at I.1.c.9.3. Wagon lines bombed, four men wounded.	

W. H. Humphrey Capt. Adjt.
186 Brigade R.F.A.

Volume II Appendix I

39th DIVISIONAL ARTILLERY

TABLE OF RELIEFS

Unit	Relieve	Gun Position	Wagon Line	Remarks
H.Q.174 Bde	Right Group	I.14.a.9.3.	G.24.b.8.8.	
A/174	A/103	I.27.b.2.8(4) I.27.b.5.3(2)	G.24.b.8.8.	
B/174	B/103	I.27.b.2.0(4) I.27.b.5.3(2)	G.24.b.8.8.	
C/174	C/103	I.15.b.35.45	G.24.b.8.8.	Take over guns stripped except for sights.
D/174	D/103	I.14.a.75.40	G.24.b.8.8.	
C/186	2 secs C/102	I.15.a.25.25. (4 guns)	H.13.c.4.6.	Comes under Right Group
		I.3.d.65.55 (2 guns)		Comes under Left Group.
H.Q.186 Bde	Left Group	I.14.b.1.8. I.8.d.30.45	H.13.a.5.9. G.10.a.9.6.	
A/186	A/102	XXXXXXXXX.		
B/186	B/102	I.8.d.3.7.	G.9.b.1.8. G.9.b.6.3.	Take over 2 guns.
D/186	D/102	I.8.c.8.3.	G.22.b.5.7.	

MARCH TABLE

174th Brigade, R.F.A.

To be clear of cross roads F.30.c.3.5. by 10 a.m.
Route Main Road through POPERINGHE and thence via
Cross Roads at G.6.d.5.1. - G.7.c.2.5.

186th Brigade, R.F.A.

To be clear of HOUTKERQUE at 10 a.m. Route via
WATOU - POPERINGHE.

KING'S BIRTHDAY HONOURS GAZETTE - 1917

Reglt No.	Rank	Name	Award	Unit.
	Lt-Colonel	C.H.Kilner	Mentioned in Despatches	H.Q. 186 Bde R.F.A.
	Lieut	V.Hill	"	"
	Capt	A.E.Delgado	"	"
41179	Bdr.	Jones A.	Distingusihed Conduct Medal	"
	2/Lieut	S.E.Lamb	Mentioned in Despatches	A/186 Bde R.F.A.
26754	Bdr.	Tynsk W.V.	"	"
	2/Lieut	D.S.Doig	Military Cross	C/186 Bde R.F.A.
38433	Sgt.	Hird J.	Mentioned in Despatches	"
	2/Lieut	Wilson G.A.	"	D/186 Bde R.F.A.
38057	Sergt	King W.J.	Military Medal	C/186 Bde R.F.A.
38362	Gunner	Mitchell R.	"	"

War Diary
186 Brigade R.F.A.
Sept. 23rd 24 Volume II

Army Form C. 2118.

186 Bgde RFA
Sheet 23   Last appendix
VOLUME II   13

WAR DIARY
or
INTELLIGENCE SUMMARY.
(Erase heading not required.)

Instructions regarding War Diaries and Intelligence Summaries are contained in F. S. Regs., Part II. and the Staff Manual respectively. Title pages will be prepared in manuscript.

Place	Date	Hour	Summary of Events and Information	Remarks and references to Appendices
ALBA	8.1.17		186 Brigade RFA were ordered to relieve the 161 Brigade 32nd Divl Artillery in positions as follows:-	
			HQrs 186 C.11.c.87.65	
			A " D.7.c.Y.Y	
			B " D.7.c.63.35	
			D.1.b.04.18 Sniping Gun	
			D.2.b.05.15 Close defence gun	
			C " C.18.b.09.55	
			D " C.12.b.6.3	
ALBERTA	11.1.17	12.30pm	The Relief took place on nights 8th/9th & 9/10th. Enemy put down heavy barrage on whole of the Divisional Front (Captured) and batteries suffered the following casualties.	
			A/186 Major P. Wright (Killed) 5 ORs wounded	
			B/186 2/Lt Wilcox (wounded) 2 ORs Killed	
IPRES	12.1.17	5.30pm	Two men of A Bty killed	
	2.1.17		Lt A.R.P.S Lanfranco and 7/Rt qf Warner joined and posted to D/186 & A/186 respectively	
ALBERTA	10.1.17		Lt E.E Jones & 2/Lt R.R.Davies joined and posted to B/186.	

Sheet 24 186 Brigade R.F.A.
Volume ﬁ Last appendix 13

WAR DIARY
or
INTELLIGENCE SUMMARY
Army Form C. 2118.

(Erase heading not required.)

Place	Date	Hour	Summary of Events and Information	Remarks and references to Appendices
ALBERTA	18.1.18		Major E.F. Spencer MC posted from the BRSR and posted to command B/186.	
"	"		Capt G.H. Barnett appointed A/Major and posted to command B/186.	
"	23.1.18	4pm	A/Bde were relieved by HQrs 23rd R.F.A. Bde and withdrew to Wagon lines at STEENTJE MILL	
"	"		HQrs Wagon line moved from H.5.d to STEENTJE MILL and Battery Wagon lines to PESELHOEK	
"	"	4pm	Batteries withdrew guns and marched to their respective Wagon lines at PESELHOEK.	
STEENTJE MILL	25.1.18		The undermentioned officers joined and were posted as follows:— 2/Lt. E.C. Yalio) to D/186 and 2/Lt A. Morgan to B/186 A/M Lawton)	
"	27.1.18		The 186 Bde R.F.A. entrained at PROVEN and proceeded to the SOMME	
"	28.1.18		The 186 Bde R.F.A. detrained at MERICOURT L'ABBÉ and marched to billets at LAHOUSSOYE	
LAHOUSSOYE	30.1.18		2/Lt. M.H. Hogg joined and posted to A/186.	

N. Hampton Capt + Adjt
186 R.F.A. Bde

Casualties

Capt C C Corbett AVC attached Hdrs 186 Bde RFA
　　　　　　　　　Died of Wounds Self Inflicted
　　　　　　　　　　　　3-2-18

Date	No.	Rank	Name		Status	Unit
11/1/18	24455	Gnr	Williams	T.H.	Wounded	B/186
	143076	"	Ogilvie	D.R.	"	"
	173926	"	Mitchell	L	"	"
	40241	D	Earley	J	"	"
	2/Lt		Wilcock	J.M.	"	D/186
	258346	Gnr	Brown	E.B.	Killed	D/186
	40166	"	Johnson	S.T.J.	"	D/186
	Major		Wright	P.	"	B/186
12/1/18	93293	Gnr	O'Brien	J	Killed	A/186

　　　　　　　　　　　　　　H. M.
　　　　　　　　　　　　　Capt & Adjt
　　　　　　　　　　　　　186 Bde RFA

186 Brigade RFA
Last Appendix
13.

Vol 24

SHEET 25

WAR DIARY
or
INTELLIGENCE SUMMARY
(Erase heading not required.)

VOLUME II

Army Form C. 2118.

Place	Date	Hour	Summary of Events and Information	Remarks and references to Appendices
LANEUVILLE	1917 Feb 2	9.45am	186 Brigade RFA marched from LANEUVILLE HAUT to camp at ALLAINES (Sht 62c T.4 central)	Appendix
ALLAINES	Feb 3	9.30am	Route MARICOURT – CLERY SUR SOMME – ALLAINES	14 Attached
"	"	"	186 Brigade RFA marched from ALLAINES HAUT to training camp at MOISLAINS (Sht 62c B12) and commenced a period of training	
MOISLAINS	Feb 12		Major G.B. Tanner joined from BASE and posted to Command A/186	
"	" 13		186 Brigade RFA marched from MOISLAINS unto Wagon Lines at NURLU	
NURLU	" 16	12.30pm	G.O.C. 4th Corps inspected the 186 Brigade RFA	
"	" 17/18		186 Brigade RFA were ordered to relieve 174 Brigade RFA in positions as follows:—	
			HQrs N.9.d.70.60	
			A/186 W.14.a.35.40	
			B/186 H.10.t.65.85 } Sheet 57c	
			C/186 H.10.c.75.73"	
			D/186 W.10.a.00.80	
	" 18		186 Brigade Wagon Lines took over wagon lines occupied by the 174 Brigade RFA at HEUDICOURT	

Army Form C. 2118.

SHEET 26   186 Brigade RFA

WAR DIARY
or
INTELLIGENCE SUMMARY.

VOLUME II

(Erase heading not required.)

Instructions regarding War Diaries and Intelligence Summaries are contained in F. S. Regs., Part II. and the Staff Manual respectively. Title pages will be prepared in manuscript.

Place	Date	Hour	Summary of Events and Information	Remarks and references to Appendices
NURLU	Feb 19		Colonel Lord R.G. Brown proceeded on leave and Major F.E Spencer MC assumed temporary command of the 186 Brigade RFA	
HEEDICOURT	" 21		2/Lt L.C Gubbins and 9/Lt A.J Applegate transferred from 186 Brigade RFA to 39 Divl Trench Mortars.	
"	" 28	6.45pm	186 Brigade RFA fired in support of infantry raid. The first (119/div)	
"	Mar 1st	5.15am	Our infantry entered enemy trenches and found them unoccupied. Second (118 Divn) was a great success, great damage being done to enemy trenches and two prisoners were captured	

J.E. Spencer
Major Cmdg
186 Bde RFA

SECRET

186th Brigade R.F.A.

War Diary   Pages 19-20
            Volume II

Vol 21

39th Div.

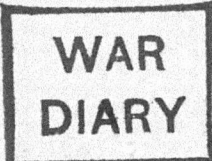

Headquarters,

186th BRIGADE, R.F.A.

M A R C H

1 9 1 8

B139
180 Brigade RHA
last appendix 14

Vol II

Army Form C. 2118.

WAR DIARY
INTELLIGENCE SUMMARY
(Erase heading not required.)

Place	Date	Hour	Summary of Events and Information	Remarks and references to Appendices
HEUDECOURT	1/3/18	10.7am	The 21st Division took over the Right Sector of the 39 Divisional front the 114 I.B. being withdrawn into Divisional Reserve.	Appendix 15
			The 39th Divisional front then extended from X.9.a.9.5 to R.20.d.2.2 Sheet 57c 1/40000 (Casualties)	
			The 21st Division being on the right and the 2nd Division on the left	
			The Artillery was reorganised into two groups the Right Group covering	
			the 110th Infantry Brigade, consisting of 150 Army Brigade RFA and 186 Bde RFA	
			under the command of Lieut Col Dixon, the Left Group covering the 118 I.B.	
			consisting of 65th Army Brigade RFA and 174 Brigade RFA under Lt-Col Brooks	
	2/3/18		Harrassing and destructive fire was kept up from dawn to midnight	
			every 24 hours commencing the 2-3-18 on the enemy defences trench and tracks	
	6/3/18	5am	The enemy raided the front held by the Right Battalion 116 I.B. one	
			prisoner was left in our hands two of our men missing	
	9th		Our artillery fired in support of two tanks showing the night 9/10th	
			at 11pm and 3am respectively, both attempts found the enemy trenches empty.	
	10/11		The 186 Bde RFA were relieved by the 57th Brigade RFA 9th Division	
			on the 10th & 11th March 1918 and marched to training area at HALLE I.9.6.5.5 sheet 62.c 1/40000	

Sheet 28   186 Brigade R.F.A.
           Volume II

Army Form C. 2118.

WAR DIARY
or
INTELLIGENCE SUMMARY.
(Erase heading not required.)

Place	Date	Hour	Summary of Events and Information	Remarks and references to Appendices
HERDECOURT	10th	10am	Placed in Corps Reserve to be ready to march at 1 hour notice and in G.H.Q. Reserve to be ready to entrain at 12 hours notice.	
MAPLE	14th	10pm	Ordered to concentrate at HAUT ALLAINES at 6am on the 15-3-18	
—	15th	5am	Marched to HAUT ALLAINES.	
HAUT ALLAINES	15th	9pm	Entered into Billets at HAUT ALLAINES at I.5.a. 0.8 with wagon lines at I.4.b.26 Sheet 62c 1/40000	
—	21st	4.45am	The enemy put down a very heavy barrage along whole of Corps Front. The 186 Brigade R.F.A. stood to until 2.30pm when orders were received to move and reinforce the 16th Div. Arty. The Brigade took up positions in a valley running between TINCOURT and LONGAVESNES (Sheet 62c) K.26 and K.3.a. N.W. of BOIS de TINCOURT covering 118 I.B.de.	
BOIS de TINCOURT	22nd	9am	The Brigade held positions until the enemy had pressed within a short distance of the guns and then retired to positions along valley in (SL 62C) K.8 & 15. Then BUSSU	
BUSSU	23rd		The Brigade retired to positions in (Sheet 62C) I.14.4.15 and covered infantry until forced to retire over SOMME by the bridge near HALLE and take up fresh positions	

186 Brigade RFA

Sheet 29
Volume II

Army Form C. 2118.

WAR DIARY
or
INTELLIGENCE SUMMARY.
(Erase heading not required.)

Place	Date	Hour	Summary of Events and Information	Remarks and references to Appendices
BUSSU	23rd		in Sheet 62c H.27,28,+ 33 HQ HERBÉCOURT E. Battery lost 1 gun hit by shell	
HERBECOURT	24th		The 186 Brigade RFA did great execution among enemy transport advancing North of SOMME. 1 Section from each battery took up an advanced position where direct observation could be obtained and fired several thousands of rounds into enemy	
"	25th		19th Corps retired. 5th Corps. The enemy forced a passage over canal and the 186 Bde RFA retired and took up positions in front of CAPPY and covered the 119 Inf Brigade	
CAPPY	26th		The 186 Brigade RFA retired to positions between MORCOURT and PROYART (Sheet 62D) Q.23 & 24 HQ MORCOURT.	
MORCOURT	27th		The 186 Brigade RFA retired to positions at LAMOT (Sk 62d) 0.36 and again to MARCELCAVE finally taking up positions in front of VILLERS BRETTONEUX (Sk 62d) 0.36 - v.6 HQ VILLERS BRETTONEUX. The 186 Brigade RFA covering front of sector held by CAREY'S FORCE South of AMIENS ROAD. C/186 suffered the following casualties to Officers 2/Lt IRVINE (Killed) 2/Lt ROBINSON (Wounded)	

186 Brigade RFA
Sheet 30 Volume II

Army Form C. 2118.

WAR DIARY
or
INTELLIGENCE SUMMARY.
(Erase heading not required.)

Instructions regarding War Diaries and Intelligence Summaries are contained in F. S. Regs., Part II. and the Staff Manual respectively. Title pages will be prepared in manuscript.

Place	Date	Hour	Summary of Events and Information	Remarks and references to Appendices
VILLERS BRETTONEUX	30/3/18		The Brigade received orders to cover sector held by the 1st Cavalry Division North of AMIENS ROAD.	
"	31/3/18		The 186 Brigade RFA came under orders of the 16th Divn Artillery and moved to positions North of AMIENS ROAD (Sh 62D.O.29.30) 4Bn PRISONERS CAGE (Sh 62D.O.27d)	

Alfred Moncrieff
Lieut Col
Cmdg 186 Brigade RFA
Capt + Adjt
186 Brigade RFA.

A P P E N D I X   15.

Casualties.

(Note: This Appendix appears to be MISSING).

39th Divisional Artillery

186th BRIGADE R. F. A.

APRIL 1918.

186 Brigade R.F.A.

SHEET 31

WAR DIARY
INTELLIGENCE SUMMARY
VOLUME II

Last Appendix 15. Vol 26

Place	Date	Hour	Summary of Events and Information	Remarks and references to Appendices
VILLERS BRET (unknown cape)	Apr 4	4:45 am	Enemy put down heavy barrage on the Front Line & Gun Line area. Enemy infantry attempted to advance under cover of this barrage but were stopped by concentrated fire from our Field Batteries and suffered tremendously in consequence. Capt Crowdy & 2/Lieut Welford of C/186 Bde were wounded & evacuated to F. Ambulance. After this operation the 186 Brigade R.F.A. moved back to positions in (Sht 62 d) O.32. H.Qrs. in CHATEAU BOIS L'ABBE O.26.c. The 186 Brigade R.F.A. move to positions in (Sht 62 d) U.1. as a sub. group under the 66th Divn Arty.	
BOIS L'ABBE	5th		H.Q. remaining at BOIS L'ABBE	
	7th		On 186 Brigade R.F.A. fired barrage in support of an attack on BOIS DE HANGARD by the 9th Australian Brigade. The attack was successful.	
	9th		Enemy attacked HANGARD without success. 300 prisoners including 1 officer being taken. Capt Curtis of B/186 wounded & evacuated.	

SHEET 33

WAR DIARY or INTELLIGENCE SUMMARY.

Army Form C. 2118.

Last appendix No 15.

Place	Date	Hour	Summary of Events and Information	Remarks and references to Appendices
BOIS L'ABBE.	Apl 10		Major G A Pellins joined from Base & posted to command 6.186.	
	11th		Major J.C. Spencer MC posted to command the 19th Brigade R.H.A.	
			The 186 Brigade R.H.A. took up new positions in front of the Bois l'ABBE	
			to the rearward on the cast of wood.	
	12th		The enemy made another determined attack on HANGARD and gained	
			possession of the village but were driven out by a counter attack	
			commencing at 7.35 P.m.	
	13th		The 186 Brigade R.H.A. withdrew from line to billets at CAGNY (Sh 62d)	
			M 21 c	
CAGNY	15th		The 186 Brigade R.H.A. marched from CAGNY to billets at BEHENCOURT	Absentees /16
BEHENCOURT	16th		The 186 Brigade R.H.A. marched from BEHENCOURT to SAULTY (VI Corps area)	/16
SAULTY	17th		The 186 Brigade R.H.A. marched from SAULTY to billets at HAUTEVILLE.	Casualties

Alfred Browne Lt Col
Commandant 186 Brigade R.H.A.

CASUALTIES APRIL

Date	Number	Name	Status	Unit
4th April.	44007	Dr. Barnard	Killed	H.Q.
	148843	Dr. Jones J.	Wounded	C/186
		Capt. E. F. Crowdy	"	"
		2/Lieut. W. Wilford		
	40221	Dr. Presho G.	Killed	"
	47903	Dr. Ebden J.H.	"	"
	17322	Dr. Weeks A.L.	"	"
	38255	Cpl. Lawson A.W.	Wounded	"
	84082	Gn. Corfield J.	"	"
	38381	Fit. Hall O.W.	"	"
		Gnr. Salt J.	"	"
	178061	Dr. Walsh H.	"	"
	2330	Dr. Bunn C.	"	"
	38294	Dr. Cave A.	"	"
	194584	Dr. Gamble J.	"	"
	786193	Gn. Holmes A.	"	"
	971164	Dr. Irvine J.E.	"	"
	43600	Dr. Kerr J.W.	"	"
	38299	Dr. Watson C.	"	"
	2644	Gn. Ward E.	Shell Shock	"
	46123	Gn. Mutimer K.	Wounded at duty	"
	42821	Gn. Hughes F.	"	"
	24	Dr. Craig R.	"	"
	24218	Gn. Moore	Killed	D/186
	20162	Cpl. Branch	Wounded	"
	10863	Bdr. Tootill	"	"
	129932	Gn. Strachan	"	"
	148125	Gn. Shackleton	"	"
	810936	Gn. Edgecock J.	Killed	A/186
	67247	Bdr. Archer	Wounded	"
	72068	Cpl. Freeman W.L.	"	B/186
	213611	Gn. Norton P.	"	"
	965140	Gn. Gray W.	"	"
	99307	Dr. Hickson T.	"	"
	43993	Sgt. Alcock C.	"	"
	233200	Dr. Colston J.H.	"	"
	177453	Gn. Low F.C.	"	"
5th April			"	"
	35577	Bd. Turton A.	Killed	"
	44065	Gn. Bullen P.	Wounded	"
	35581	Gn. Whittington W.	Killed	C/186
	1919	Sgt. Strachan J.	Wounded	"
	104789	Gn. Reddington W.	"	"
	33785	Dr. Robertson A.	"	"
	38423	Sgt. Hirl J.	Wounded at duty	"
	117302	Bd. Allen W.	"	"
6th April	21955	Gn. Shaddock M.	Wounded	A/186
	705693	Gn. Taylor R.	"	"
	26690	L/Bd. Carey R.	Wounded at duty	"
	215644	Gn. Kirkpatrick S.	"	"
	31969	Cpl. Walker S.J.	Wounded	B/186
	95694	Gn. Allan G.	"	D/186
7th April	215644	Gn. Kirkpatrick S.	"	A/186
	143449	Bd. McGilvary A.	"	B/186
	149247	Gn. Simkins F.	"	"
	836126	Gn. Wilmott W.	"	"
	31931	L/Bd. McClughen G.	"	"
	38047	Gn. Wells A.G.	"	"
	46038	Dr. McDade H.	"	D/186
	42988	Dr. Wilson	"	"
	176335	Dr. Woodford A.	"	"

-2-

Date	Number	Name	Status	Unit
8th April	2/Lieut W.Garbutt		Wounded at duty	A/186
	46399	Bd. T. McGregor	Killed	B/186
	11537	Gn. Taylor J.S.	Wounded	B/186
	214217	Gn. Keylock W.J.	"	"
	31873	Dr. Dishart A.D.	"	"
	31887	Dr. Fryer C.W.	"	"
	19966	Dr. Slade J.	Wounded at duty	"
	38392	Dr. Hewitt H.W.	Wounded	C/186
	285688	Dr. Spicer A.F.G.	"	"
9th April	243147	Gn. Aird J.	Killed	"
	103206	Gn. Hedges P.	Wounded	"
	189547	Gn. Alcock Hackett W.	"	"
	1648	Gn. Alcock J.S.	"	"
	38318	Dr. Banfill W.	"	"
	38392	Dr. Hewitt H.	"	"
	1988	Dr. Spicer A.T.J.	"	"
	117302	Bd. Allen W.	"	"
	102163	Gn. Drayton W.J.	"	"
	217075	Dr. Rish B.	Killed	B/186
	38099	Dr. Bryan W.	Wounded	"
	180541	Dr. West W.J.	Killed	"
		Capt W.B. Carter	Wounded	"
11th April	211520	Dr. Taylor H.E.	"	"
	697037	Dr. Isaacs B.	"	"
	786092	Dr. Scholefield J.	S. Shock	
12th April	26700	Gn. Brackenboro G.	Killed	A/186
	3248	Gn. Lawliss	W. Gassed	"
13th April	80547	L/Bd. Rylands W.	Wounded	D/186
	217589	Gn. Carrigan G.	"	"
	25436	Gn. Davies J.	"	"
	38316	Gn. Wickham R.	"	"
	160352	Gn. Gooding R.	"	"
	93799	Tpr. Williams A.J.	Wounded at duty	"
	74202	Bd. Pratt H.	Wounded	C/186
	801885	Gn. Thomas H.V.	"	"
	249181	Gn. Howard A.	"	"
	31857	Dr. Bain	"	A/186
	681831	Gn. Odgers J.	"	"
	75127	Gn. England F.	"	"
	961708	Fit. Bastick A.P.	Killed	B/186
	730501	Gn. Cummings B.	Wounded	"
	58146	L/Bd. Goodhew E.A.	"	"

COPY

The C.R.A. wishes to thank all officers, N.C.O's and men of the 39th Divisional Artillery and Signal Section R.E. attached for their magnificent work since 21st March — the conduct of all ranks throughout has been up to the highest traditions of the Royal Regiment of Artillery and the value of their work beyond estimation.

Being the last troops to be withdrawn from the line who started fighting on 21st March all ranks have thoroughly earned whatever rest they can be spared for. The work is however not yet finished and when re-equipped he knows everyone will be ready to continue the destruction of the enemy whereever called on.

14th April, 1918.

(sd) M. Thornycroft,
Brigade Major, R.A.,
39th Divisional Artillery.,

Army Form C. 2118.

WAR DIARY
or
INTELLIGENCE SUMMARY.

Sheet 34   Volume II   186 Brigade RFA

Place	Date	Hour	Summary of Events and Information	Remarks and references to Appendices
HAUTEVILLE	30.4.18		The 186 Brigade RFA moved to Billets at BASSEUX. HQrs remaining at HAUTEVILLE.	Appendix No 14
"	1.5.18		The 186 Brigade RFA marched to wagon lines vacated by the 18th AFA Brigade located as follows:-	Attached (Casualties)
			A/186 R.22.a.6.4	
			B/186 R.22.b.1.5	
			C/186 R.16.c.4.8 } Sheet 51c	
			D/186 R.16.c.2.9	
		NIGHTS 30/4/18 1/5/18 1/5/18 2/5/18	The 186 Brigade RFA relieved the 18th AFA Brigade in positions as follows:-	
			A/186 M.15.b.95.35	
			B/186 M.14.b.33.05 } Sheet 51c	
			C/186 M.14.d.40.65	
			D/186 M.15.b.85.93	
AGNY	2.6.18		HQrs 186 Brigade RFA relieved the HQrs 18th RFA Brigade in positions as follows:- Wagon Line R.16.c.4.8 - Gun line M.13.b.45.15 Sheet 51c The 186 Brigade RFA came under orders of O.C. Left Group 2nd Canadian Div.Arty.	

Sheet 35
Volume II

WAR DIARY
or
INTELLIGENCE SUMMARY.

186 Bgde RFA

Army Form C. 2118.

(Erase heading not required.)

Place	Date	Hour	Summary of Events and Information	Remarks and references to Appendices
AGNY	May 14/15	15/16	A/186 and D/186 Batteries were transferred to the Right Group and relieved C and D/181 respectively in position and wagon lines as follows:—	Ref Sheets 51.8 & c 1/20000
			Wagon Lines	
			A/186 { S.1.b.28.15 (2 guns) R.22.d.9.1	
			{ X.5.d.70.62 (4 — —)	
			D/186 { X.11.d.44.93 (4 — —) R.16.c.2.9	
			{ X.4.d.99.60 (2 — —)	
—	16th		HQrs 186 Brigade RFA were relieved by HQrs 18th AFA Brigade and withdrawn taking over billets occupied by HQrs 181 Brigade RFA at BEAUMETZ-LES-LOGES.	
—	19th		The following officers joined and were posted to Batteries as follows:—	
			Lieut P.K. Stirling and 2/Lieut H.E.B. Pratt to A/186 Brigade RFA	
			2/Lieut N Duncan and 2/Lieut J.L. Allen to B/186 " "	
			2/Lieut J.L. Gibbon to C/186 " "	
BEAUMETZ	24		Major P.H. Evans-Gwynne D.S.O. joined from BASE and posted to command B/186 Brigade RFA with effect from 25.5.17 vice Major E.W. Clarke evacuated sick	
—	27		2/Lieut P.H.B. Amon joined and posted to D/186 Brigade RFA	

Stephens Lieut T. L. Creevy
Comdg 186 Bde RFA

Sheet. 36.   *See appendix 17*

WAR DIARY
or
INTELLIGENCE SUMMARY: 186 Bde R.F.A
(Erase heading not required.)

Army Form C. 2118.

Place	Date	Hour	Summary of Events and Information	Remarks and references to Appendices
BEAUMETZ	5/78		2nd Lieut C. C. Crane transferred to 174 Brigade R.F.A.	Appendix 18
-"-	21/6/18		2/Lieut A.W.H. Beaumont joined 186 Brigade R.F.A & posted to C/186.	*casualties*
-"-	22/6/18		The 186 Brigade R.F.A was withdrawn from the line	
PAS	25/6/18		The 186 Brigade R.F.A joined with IV Corps & marched to Wagon lines at PAS, & was placed in Mobile Reserve.	
COUIN.	29/6/18		Marched to Wagon lines at COUIN (Sheet 57 D.)	
	30/6/18		Mobile Training	

Nov. for Lt. Col. R.F.A.
Comdg 186 Brigade R.F.A.

Sheet 37.

VOLUME II

Last Appendix 17.

186th Brigade R.F.A.

Army Form C. 2118.

WAR DIARY
INTELLIGENCE SUMMARY.
(Erase heading not required.)

Place	Date	Hour	Summary of Events and Information	Remarks and references to Appendices
COUIN	July 5th		The 186th Brigade received orders to entrain for the II Corps area & move took place as follows:- H.Qrs, C & D Batteries entrained at DOULLENS & detrained at PROVEN. A & B Batteries entrained at MONDICOURT & detrained at REXPOEDE, afterwards the whole Brigade marched to Bulleh & Wagon Lines at ST JAN TER BIEZEN.	Aberdeen H Cannalton
ST JAN TER BIEZEN	July 6th		1 Section gun Battery of the 186th Brigade occupied positions covering the Boot Poperinghe System.	
" "	July 7th		On the night of the 7/8th July 1917 the 186th Brigade R.F.A. received orders to reinforce the 33rd Div Arty 9 took up positions as follows:— No. 3 Group covering the Left Brigade Wagon Line. Forward Wagon Line	
			H.Qrs. H.10.a.6.6.	
			A/186. H.11d.9.2. } 2 guns H.17d.60.45 } Sheet A/186 A.14.b.0.2. A/186 B.3.a.6.6.	
			B/186. H.17a.9.3. } 2 guns H.11c.9.3. } 28 NW B/186 A.8.d.5.3. B/186 B.2.a.0.4.	
			C/186. 4 guns H.17.0.9.3 C/186 F.28.d. C/186 A.30.d.5.4.	
			D/186. 4 Hows. H.17.d.0.3 D/186 F.28.d. D/186 B.19.a.3.6.	

Sheet. 38.

WAR DIARY
or
INTELLIGENCE SUMMARY.
(Erase heading not required.)

VOLUME II.

186th Brigade R.F.A.

Army Form C. 2118.

Place	Date	Hour	Summary of Events and Information	Remarks and references to Appendices
VLAMERTINGHE	July 14	2:25 am	The 186th Brigade R.F.A. fired a barrage in support of raid by the Left Bank. The barrage was a great success but enemy had evacuated trenches & no personnel was taken.	
"	"	6 am	The Brigade fired in support of an attack on original Front Line at VOORMEZEELE. The attack was a complete surprise and all objectives were taken with 7 Officers & 313 O.Rks.	
VLAMERTINGHE CHATEAU.	July 16 21. 30/31.		H.Qrs 186 Brigade R.F.A. moved to Vlamertinghe Chateau. 2/Lieut A. McNab returned from the Base & posted to A/186 Bde R.F.A. Two sections of battery of the 186th Bde R.F.A. were relieved by the 174th Bde R.F.A. & withdrawn to Wagon Lines	
	31/1 Aug.		The remaining sections were relieved & withdrawn to Wagon Lines The 186th Bde R.F.A. marched to DROGLANDT & occupied billets & wagon lines as follows:— Sheet 27.	
			A/186. J.6.c.6.0. J.6.c.8.4. J.6.c.8.4. B/186. J.11.b.6.4. J.11.a.9.4. C/186. J.5.c.3.7. J.11.a.6.9. D/186. J.4.b.6.7. J.4.a.3.8. H.Qrs. K.8.a.o.o.	

- CASUALTIES -

JULY - 1918.

18/7/18	120167 Gnr. Mullins F.E.	A/186	Wounded
25/7/18	890642 Bdr. Ginn J.B.	C/186	Wounded
16/7/18	129947 Gnr. Devaney F.	"	"
	84247 Gnr. Batey C.	"	"
	154315 Dr. Parsons H.	"	Killed
	243081 Dr. MacIntoch C.	"	Wounded. At duty.
25/7/18	38441 Bdr. Capeling A.E.	"	Wounded.
	20514 Gnr. Thompson J.	"	"
	945356 Gnr. Marsden G.H.	"	"
	53683 Gnr. Hinks F.	"	"
	47595 Dr. Crout J.H.	"	"
	249466 Dr. Boyles W.	"	Wounded. At duty.
26/7/18	810062 Cpl. Hale W.	B/186	Wounded
	112107 Gnr. Nicholson G.	"	"

Capt. & Adjt.,
186th Brigade, R.F.A.,

31st July, 1918.

186 Brigade RFA   WAR DIARY   Army Form C. 2118.
Sheet 39   or INTELLIGENCE SUMMARY.
Last appendix 18

Place	Date	Hour	Summary of Events and Information	Remarks and references to Appendices
DROGLANDT	Aug 5th		The 186 Brigade RFA marched to the XV Corps area and occupied wagon lines and billets at RACRUINGHEM. 149m at BELLE CROIX.	
BELLE CROIX	" 6th		The 186 Brigade RFA commenced a period of training.	
—	" 15th	7 p.m.	The 186 Brigade RFA marched to wagon lines at LA BREARDE (Sheet 27 V.5.c.5.1) and came under orders of the 9th Divisional Artillery. HQ 186 Bde Gun line Sheet 27 W.5.A.2.3	
FLETRE	Night 15/16th		The 186 Brigade RFA placed two flank guns for battery into action in forward positions as follows:—	
			A/186 X.7.a.90.30	
			B/186 X.7.b.20.50 } Sheet 27	
			C/186 X.7.b.60.35	
			B/186 W.12.d.90.85	
—	16/17		Remainder of Guns taken into action and ammunition dumped.	
—	19th	3 am	The 186 Brigade RFA fired a barrage in support of an attack by the 9th and 29th Divisions. All objectives were taken on time and special compliment paid to excellent barrage put down by the 186 Brigade RFA	

Army Form C. 2118.

186 Brigade RFA   Sheet 40

WAR DIARY
or
INTELLIGENCE SUMMARY.
(Erase heading not required.)

Place	Date	Hour	Summary of Events and Information	Remarks and references to Appendices
FLETRE	20th	11am	Enemy counter attacked on right of our front without success.	
			The attack involved high ground between METEREN and OUTERSTEENE.	
			865 prisoners were captured during the operations	
	21st		The 186 Brigade RFA were withdrawn to wagon lines	
LA BREDE	22/23		The 186 Brigade RFA entrained at ARQUES and detrained at AUBIGNY and	
			marched to billets and wagon lines at ACQ	
ACQ	night 23/24		Forward wagon lines were established at CITADEL ARRAS and batteries	
			commenced dumping ammunition in positions selected for occupation.	
			The 186 Bde wagon lines moved to the CITADEL ARRAS and after dark batteries	
			placed their guns in positions as follows :-	
			A/186 M.6.a.57.51	
			B/186 M.6.a.57.65 HQrs Tunnels G.29.c.8.8	
			C/186 G.36.c.91.48	
			D/186 M.6.a.90.72	
ARRAS	25		Guns placed in action and remainder of ammunition dumped.	
	26	3 am	The 186 Brigade RFA fired a barrage in support of an attack by the	

186 Brigade RFA WAR DIARY or INTELLIGENCE SUMMARY.
Sheet 41
Army Form C. 2118.

(Erase heading not required.)

Place	Date	Hour	Summary of Events and Information	Remarks and references to Appendices
ARRAS	Aug 26		2nd Canadian Division and covering the 5th Brigade.	
			The attack progressed and batteries advanced to positions in (Sheet 51B)	
			H.35.d. HQrs H.35.c.8.6.	
TILLOY H.35.c.8.6	"27		The 186 Brigade RFA moved forward to positions on (Sheet 51B) N.24.c	
			HQrs N.23.c.8.4 Wagon lines 16 N.3.4	
	"27	10am	Colonel The Lord Alfred Browne DSO killed in action.	
			Major A.H. Evans- Gwynne DSO }	
			2nd Lieut G.L. Allen } D/186 wounded	
			Major J.H. Fairbanks took over command of the 186 Brigade RFA	
NANCOURT	"28	3pm	B+C/186 Brigade RFA moved and took up positions in valley O.20. O.25	
			(Sheet 51B)	
		3pm	Colonel The Lord Alfred Browne DSO buried at DAINVILLE	
			Major H.B. Teleng M.C. of C/186 wounded at duty	
	29		D/186 Brigade moved forward to valley in Sheet 51B O.20.	
	30	4.40pm	The 186 Bde RFA fired a barrage in support of an attack by the	
			1st Canadian Division	

Army Form C. 2118.

186 Brigade RFA WAR DIARY
Sheet 42   or
INTELLIGENCE SUMMARY.

(Erase heading not required.)

Instructions regarding War Diaries and Intelligence Summaries are contained in F. S. Regs., Part II. and the Staff Manual respectively. Title pages will be prepared in manuscript.

Place	Date	Hour	Summary of Events and Information	Remarks and references to Appendices
WANCOURT	Aug 30		A Bty B/186 moved forward immediately after attack to positions in front of CHERISY. H Bn in trench O.31.b (Sheet 57B)	See Appendix 18. Casualties
	31		C/186 moved forward to a position in front of CHERISY	Appendix 19 Casualties

K Hemphill Lt Colonel RFA
Comdg 186 Brigade RFA

Appendix 19 - Casualties
August 1918

26798	Dr Fitzgerald DL	A/186	Wounded	27-8-18
90165	Dr Rooney J		Missing	
	Lt-Col Lord Alfred Browne D.S.O	HQ/186	Killed	
	Major A.H. Evans-Gwynne DSO	D/186	Wounded	
	2/Lieut G.L. Allen			
210414	L/Bdr Nash AW			
41609	Dr Stanton J			
	Major H.B. Telling MC	C/186	W. at duty	28-8-18
177641	Gnr Murtagh JJ	B/186	Wounded	29-8-18
49676	" Denham RJ	D/186	Killed	30-8-18
215027	" Pearson HA		Wounded	
41920	Dr Luck J			
263136	Gnr Garner J		W (Gassed)	
112552	Bdr Hughes G	B/186	Wounded	31-8-18
78973	Gnr Reynolds A			
112107	" Nicholson E			
	Lieut E.B. Wheeler	C/186		
31938	Sgt Pitt CE	A/186		30-8-18
50089	" Kell H			
26691	Gnr Abbott HH			
237107	" Norman HS			
429925	Pnr Duff WJ	HQ/186	Killed	

Attached from 39 Divl Signals

95811	Dr Boynes N	Killed	C/186	31-8-18
76784	" Webb M	Wounded		
4253	" Grogan W			
220988	" Branch CF			
604391	Gnr Greenshields J	W (Gassed)		

186 Bgde RFA
Sheet 44H

Last Appendix
No. 20.

Army Form C. 2118.

WAR DIARY
or
INTELLIGENCE SUMMARY.
(Erase heading not required.)

Place	Date	Hour	Summary of Events and Information	Remarks and references to Appendices
CHERISY	Sept 1st		Colonel R.C. Reeves D.S.O. joined from 32nd Divl Arty and took over Command of the 186th Bde.	Appendix
			R.F.A. Major Fairbanks MC returned to Command A/174 Bde RFA.	21 Casualties
			The 186 Brigade RFA received orders to advance and took up positions in V.1.6.d (Sheet 51B SE) HQ. U.6.b.80.30 (Sheet 51B SN)	attached
V.6.b.80.30	2nd		The Brigade again advanced and the following positions were occupied covering crossings of the CANAL du NORD and acting under orders of the Left Group.	
			HQ 186 V.10.b.5.5 Wagon lines V.9.a	
			A/186 V.11.a.90.25	
			B/186 V.12.a.76.18 } V.1 and 2	
			C/186 V.11.d	
			D/186 V.18.a.3.2	
			Forward guns were placed in positions for enfying purposes as follows:—	
			(A/186 (1gun W.7.a.) (B/186 (1gun W.7.d.90.40) (C/186 (1gun W.7.d.98.60)	
	Night 13/14 14/15		The 186 Brigade RFA were relieved by the 52nd RFA Brigade switches to Wagon lines.	
N.10.b.5.5	15th		The 186 Brigade RFA marched to Wagon lines and Billets in the ACHICOURT Area	
			HQ A/186 B/186 +D/186 occupying CITADEL and grounds ARRAS. C/186 – AGNY.	

Army Form C. 2118.

186 Brigade RFA

WAR DIARY
or
INTELLIGENCE SUMMARY

Sheet 45

(Erase heading not required.)

Instructions regarding War Diaries and Intelligence Summaries are contained in F. S. Regs., Part II. and the Staff Manual respectively. Title pages will be prepared in manuscript.

Place	Date	Hour	Summary of Events and Information	Remarks and references to Appendices
	Sept			
ARRAS	22nd		The 186 Brigade RFA received orders to prepare positions in BUISSY N13 & rd. Sheet 51B. Forward Wagon lines were established and ammunition was dumped in accordance with instructions from the 1st Canadian Divl Artillery.	
	26th		The 186 Brigade RFA occupied above positions	
BUISSY	27th	5.20am	The 186 Brigade RFA fired a barrage in support of attack and at 6pm moved forward and took up positions in Valley N23.d. Sheet 51B.	
N23.d	28th		The attack progressed and the 186 Brigade RFA moved to a rendezvous in X.14 central and later took up positions as follows:-	
			148/186 X.8.a.20.80	
			17/186 X.8.c.central	
			B/186 X.8.b.45.44	
			C/186 X.2.d.60.10	
			D/186 X.2.c.90.13	
X.8.a.20.80	Sept 29th	8.17am	The 186 Brigade RFA fired barrage in support of attack	

K. Kenyon/r. Lt-Col RFA
Comm 186 Bde RFA

Appendix 21 - Casualties

Date	Number	Rank	Name	Status	Unit
4.9.18	216685	Dr	H.W.C. Smith	Wounded	D/186
6.9.18	116265	Gnr	T. Reeder	—	B/186
7.9.18		2/Lt	H.E.B. Pratt	W (Gassed)	—
	—	Gr. S	Pershing	—	—
	29703	Fitter	Jaeger	—	—
	73064	Gnr	Sellers	—	—
	195954	"	Smith T	—	—
	645776	"	Smith H	—	—
	72239	"	Jameson	—	—
	895404	Bdr	Boldin	—	—
	195839	Gnr	Nash	—	—
	237066	"	Boyle	—	—
	29263	"	Spencer	—	—
	4813	"	Mount	—	—
	254014	"	Mudd	—	—
	936054	"	Manock	—	—
	687002	"	Davis	—	—
	745873	"	Donovan	—	—
	207853	"	Wren	—	—
	785801	"	Sayles	—	—
	15728	"	Dennison	—	—
	242922	"	Lloyd	—	—
	226998	"	Petty	—	—
	152834	"	Parker	—	—
	87479	"	Goodman	—	—
	38423	Sgt	Hurd J	—	—
	449612	Gnr	Walker	—	—
		Major	N.B.Telling	—	—
26.9.18	64272	Dr	Bibby J	Killed	C/186
	253777	"	Belcher H	—	—
	38367	Cpl	Mitchell R	Wounded	—
	148858	L/Bdr	Moon J	—	—
	121977	Cpl	Leglt T	W (Gassed)	—
	166374	Gnr	O'Donnell	—	—
	43412	"	Dobson	—	—
	127642	Gnr	Jones G.F.	Wounded	HQ/186
28.9.18	22927	Sgt	Lanvin W	—	A/186
	26780	Bdr	Vosper P	—	—
	223226	Gnr	Sweeney P	—	—
	685956	"	Edwards A	—	—
	231976	Dr	Addyman F.	—	C/186
	242120	Gnr	Peers J	Killed	—
		Lieut	W. Fuller	N at duty	A/186
	57352	Sgt	Mahaffey R	—	—
	26799	Gnr	Roberts O.T	Wounded	—
	99457	Sgt	Candlery J.T	—	—
	134712	Gnr	Haydon H	—	—
	102153	Dr	Webb M.T	—	A/186
	1183	"	Thornton J	—	—
	117697	"	Stubbs B	—	—
	93799	Gnr	Williams A.G	—	D/186
	220697	"	Poole J	—	A/186

P.T.O

28.9.18	215288	Dvr Jones E6-2	Killed	C/186
	38398	" Macklin P.	"	"
29.9.18	810503	Gnr Whelan W	"	"
	4972	Dvr Buxton H.P.	Wounded	"
	6780	Sgt MacPherson D	"	A/186
	175854	Gnr Mitchell P.	"	"
	25828	" Moran T	"	"

30/9/18

H C Kemp Lt Col RFA
Comdg 186 Bde RFA

Army Form C. 2118.

186 Brigade RFA WAR DIARY Sheet 46
or
INTELLIGENCE SUMMARY. Last appendix 21.
(Erase heading not required.)

Place	Date	Hour	Summary of Events and Information	Remarks and references to Appendices
	Oct 8th		The 186 Brigade RFA moved and took up positions S. of RAILLEN COURT	Appendix 22 (Casualties)
			Hdrs RAILLENCOURT	
	-- 9th	4am	The 186 Brigade RFA fired a barrage in support of attack on CAMBRAI.	Appendix 23 (Honours and Awards)
			The attack proved successful and our troops entered CAMBRAI.	
	-- 11th		The 186th Brigade RFA marched to Wagon lines at PICKRENCHIE and Cabie	
			Took up positions at ESNAPS	
	-- 12th	0900	The 186 Brigade RFA fired barrage in support of an attack and then	
			moved forward to positions S. of AVESNES LE SEC.	
	-- 13th		The 186 Brigade RFA fired concentrations in support of an attack by	
			152nd Bde 51st Division.	
			Lt Colonel R.C. Rome D.S.O. wounded in action.	
	-- 14th		With the exception of C/186 the 186 Brigade R.F.A. withdrew to positions	
			at IWNY	
	-- 20th		The 186th Brigade RFA advanced and took up positions at NOVELLES	
	-- 24th		The 186th Brigade RFA advanced and took up positions in J.31.d S&.51.A.	
			N/4000.	

Army Form C. 2118.

186 Brigade RFA WAR DIARY SHEET 47

INTELLIGENCE SUMMARY.

(Erase heading not required.)

Place	Date	Hour	Summary of Events and Information	Remarks and references to Appendices
	6622		Enemy barrages were fired at 0900, 1130 and 1530	
	-23		" " " " " 1900, 1600 and 2330.	
	-24		The 186 Brigade RFA fired barrage in support of an attack on MAING and Extn. moved to position at THIANT.	
	-25	0700	The 186 Brigade RFA fired barrage in support of an attack on FAMARS.	
		1200	The 186 Brigade RFA withdrew to wagon lines at NOYELLES and DOUCHY	
	-30		The 186 Brigade came ordered into action in position near MAING. A barrage was fired in support of an attack on VARENCIENNES on the morning of the 31st	

R Rogers
Lt Colonel RFA
Comg 186 Brigade RFA

Casualties for October.

No.	Rank	Name	Unit	Status	Date
916	Dr.	Lyons W.	C/186	Killed in action	2.10.18
945816	"	Gee J.R.	D/186	do	1.10.18
41781	S/S	Ireland J.	do	do	4.10.18
	Lt	Wilam G.A.	do	Wounded	10.10.18
L/18894	L/Bdr	Sykes G.	A/186	Killed in Action	13.10.18
681831	Gnr	Odgen J.	do	do	do
7242	L/Bdr	Simpson F.	do	Wounded	do
190332	Gnr	Shore A	do	Wounded (Gassed)	15.10.18
682047	Dr.	McGuinness A.	do	Wounded	13.10.18
64753	"	Murphy J.	do	do	do
28237	Sgt	Gummer H	do	do	do
	2/Lt	Dewar F.W.	B/186	do	do
89103	Cpl	Driscoll M	do	do	do
70348	do	Jacques C	do	do	do
38063	L/Bdr	Smith W.	do	Killed in action	do
38200	Bdr	Hoskins J.	do	Wounded	do
149247	do	Simkins F.	do	do	do
38044	L/Bdr	White A.R	do	do	do
230199	Gnr	Stowill J.W.	do	do	do
19505	do	Roberts W	do	do	do
112239	do	Armes J.	do	do	do
227730	do	Hetchell J.P.	do	do	do
696936	do	Robinson C.A	do	do	do
12309	do	Stewart A	do	do	do
96216	do	McHugh J	do	do	do
840412	do	Hunt H	do	do	do
687002	do	Davies H	do	Killed in action	do
74954	do	Thompson G.	do	do	do
750593	do	Thompson J.L.	do	do	do
700838	do	Holden G.	do	Wounded	do
26768	do	Minnitt W.A.	do	do	do
202646	do	Foley C.	do	do	do
89480	do	Dobson J.W.	do	do	do
755322	Sgt	Stephenson	do	do	do
40064	Dr	Rutherford H	do	do	do
31980	do	Young W	do	do	do

2

865700	Gnr	Gregory R	B/186	Wounded	15-10-18
134215	Dr	East F.	C/186	do	13-10-18
205815	"	Logan J.	do	do	do
38432	Gnr	Wright WC	do	do	do
47702	"	Powell J	do	do	14-10-18
232910	"	King A.	D/186	Killed in action	13-10-18
945374	"	Spalding W	do	Wounded	do
148556	L/Bdr	Graham J.	do	do	do
138694	Bdr	Tye J.	do	do	do
86241	L/Bdr	Willbank A.S.	A/186	Wounded (Gassed)	19-10-18
26790	Gnr	Brooker WB	do	do	20-10-18
	2/Lt	MacNab	do	Wounded	24-10-18
	2Lt	Milward FJ	D/186	Killed in action	23-10-18
2478	Ftr	Taylor D	do	Wounded	24-10-18
700620	Gnr	Dalton F.	do	do	do
274398	"	Walker RE	do	do	do
47493	"	Bowes R.	A/186	Killed in action	25-10-18
89554	"	Chadwick JF	do	Wounded (Gassed)	25-10-18
	2/Lt	J.E. Colesby	do	do	do
2478	Ftr	Taylor D	D/186	Wounded	24-10-18
700620	Gnr	Dalton F	do	do	do
	2/Lt	Muirhead	do	Wounded (Gassed)	do

Awards for October

Bar to M.M.

L-38362 Cpl Mitchell R. M.M.   C/186

M.M.

312090 Cpl Ashcroft R.   HQ/186
22927 Sgt Scrivens W.   A/186
114988 Gnr. Stephenson J.   B/186
38063 L/Bdr Smith W.   B/186
112552 Bdr. Hughes G.   B/186
134215 Dvr East F.   C/186
35690 Gnr Kinley S.   C/186
224392 Gnr Walker A.E.   D/186

WAR DIARY
or
INTELLIGENCE SUMMARY

186 Brigade RFA
Sheet 48 that Appendix 23
Volume II

Army Form C.2118

Place	Date	Hour	Summary of Events and Information	Remarks and references to Appendices
MAING	Nov 1/3	4ᵗʰ	In action attached to 22nd Corps.	Appendices
FAYMONT		4/30	Marched to FAYMONT resting in VIII Corps Reserve.	2Lt (Honours) and Rewards
			In VIII Corps Reserve.	

[signature]
Lt Colonel RA
Comdg 186 Brigade RFA

Appendix 24 Honours & Awards.

224392 Gnr A.E. Walker   D/186.   Military Medal.
                                    6-11-18.

2/Lieut F.S. Tocher   B/186   Military Cross
                                    30-11-18

186 Bde RFA

Sheet 49.

Volume V

Vol 34

WAR DIARY
INTELLIGENCE SUMMARY.
Last appendix 24

Place	Date	Hour	Summary of Events and Information	Remarks and references to Appendices
FAVMONT	17/3/18		B. Battery 186 Brigade RFA marched from VERCHIN and rejoined the 186th Brigade RFA at FAVMONT. The 186th Brigade RFA. in VIII Corps Reserve.	

[signature]
Lt. Col. RFA
Comdg 186th Brigade RFA

www.ingramcontent.com/pod-product-compliance
Lightning Source LLC
Chambersburg PA
CBHW081553160426
43191CB00011B/1921